The Stage of Time

Secrets of the Past, the Nature of Reality,
and the Ancient Gods of History

Matthew LaCroix

DEDICATION

The Stage of Time is dedicated to all of those unique souls who have the courage to follow the difficult road of uncovering and understanding the truth, no matter what the cost. This book would never have been possible without the love and overwhelming support given from so many incredible people I have met across the course of my lifetime.

CONTENTS

ACKNOWLEDGMENTS

There are far too many people who have inspired and helped me to fully mention here but I would like to give special thanks to: Colleen Forsyth, Ann LaCroix, Nancy Jarvis, Ben Finney, Gil Croy, Robert Temple, Barbara Marciniak, Robert Bauval, Randall Carlson, Lloyd Pye, Mark Passio, Manly P. Hall, Billy Carson, Gerald Clark, Graham Hancock, Robert Schoch, Stephanie Dalley, George Smith, Jeffery Wilson, and Brien Foerster.

CHAPTER 1

CONSCIOUSNESS AND THE NATURE OF REALITY

Cultures across the world have left behind extensive evidence in ancient texts, monuments, and megalithic structures explaining that long ago, advanced civilizations once existed on the Earth that were eventually destroyed by devastating global cataclysms. These lost civilizations understood the secrets of energy, consciousness, mathematics, and even the nature of reality. This knowledge greatly contradicts the mainstream viewpoint that's been given by *certain* academics and so-called leading experts in their field, who fiercely guard the tightly controlled narrative of history. Throughout the course of this book, I will be going into extensive details to explain both why this knowledge is considered forbidden, as well as who has been hiding it. This sad and unfortunate outcome has led to great confusion throughout society, due to generations of clever conditioning over what the truth is surrounding the fundamentals of reality, ancient history, and sentient life in the universe. This was accomplished through the means of controlling key pieces of evidence, which is either destroyed or locked away in secure locations, such as the Vatican Archives, where it's rarely seen by the public.

Before anyone rolls their eyes at the idea of hidden secrets and organized conspiracies, I would like to strongly point out that none of the conclusions presented in this book are based on conjecture or faulty reasoning. Rather, this information is the result of extensive research using all available evidence in order to objectively obtain logical conclusions. It's important to remember that if certain concepts aren't presented in a progressive and organized fashion, the individual almost always rejects them. Based on that mindset and the complexity of this information, I would ask that the reader hold back any preconceived judgment until after they've finished the book. As always, remember to remain objective with everything in your life, including these words.

Ever since I was young, I've been fascinated by the universe and the nature of reality. Even from an early age, I found myself constantly questioning everything as I struggled to make sense of religion, consciousness, evolution, and the secrets of the past. Due to my intense curiosity and high levels of energy, I often had difficulty fitting in and relating to many of my peers. This led me to spend a considerable amount of time hiking and exploring the outdoors. From studying the different types of flora and fauna, all the way to geography, geology, history, and astronomy, I was eager to learn as much as I could to try and make sense of the world around me. I frustratingly couldn't understand why so many others didn't share my level of enthusiasm. It became apparent that there existed a far more expansive and almost hidden reality that was somehow invisible to most. Quickly I began to recognize the perfect harmony and intelligent design that could be seen within all of nature, represented through the golden ratio and hexagonal honeycomb.

Despite these important connections I was making, I still had a lot of questions that needed answers. I realized that I wasn't going to find all those answers on my own or in school, so I traded in my walking stick for books, and began studying ancient history and the universe. It was at that point that I came to shockingly discover that so much of what I was learning about was being *deliberately* hidden and suppressed from the public. This prompted me to ask the question of why all this information was being kept secret. That answer has fundamentally changed my life forever and set me down the long road of discovering what the truth is.

The first area of confusion to shed light on is how to accurately define the human experience. Is our true identity based on nothing more than a fleeting physical existence in a mortal body, where death only leads to darkness? Or are we defined as eternal energy that's having a physical experience through consciousness? This important question has dominated the minds of many of the philosophers and physicists throughout history and is still hotly debated today. My hope is that after reading this book, the answer to this fundamental question will become much clearer. Remember, ancient history holds *all* the answers.

The Stage of Time is intended for the expansive and

open-minded thinker, whose curiosity and dedication towards integrating new information doesn't fall victim to the conformed thoughts of those around them. These unique individuals will often forge their own path in life, despite the overwhelming challenges they face in doing so. I would like to point out that I don't pretend to have all the answers, and always strive to remain open to incorporating any new evidence or theories that come along. The most important thing above all else is to always remain objective with everything in your life and to never allow your emotions or personal bias dictate your conclusions. This can lead to a stagnation of new ideas which can often act as a blocking mechanism towards understanding new information. The famous philosopher Aristotle once said, "It is the mark of an educated mind to be able to entertain a thought without accepting it."

A personal saying that I frequently use to help explain this thought process for achieving higher levels of consciousness and a greater understanding of the world around us is, "always be aware of the level of your awareness." This seemingly simple phrase has the power to free the subconscious mind from the chains that can limit its growth and ability to see the bigger picture. That means that the most difficult obstacle that often stands in the way of an individual expanding their consciousness is their *own* logical mind. How could that be? The reason is that most of society has been largely taught through a greatly antiquated and mundane education system, that has conditioned people for generations to reject new ideas that challenge this tightly controlled narrative.

Over time, this conditioning can create what is known as "mental blocks" within us, which seek to maintain and protect the status of how we perceive reality and our purpose in life. When new information comes along that disrupts this delicate paradigm, the natural response of the individual is often to push that negative feeling away and ignore it. That perfectly normal reaction acts as the main blocking mechanism behind absorbing new ideas and information.

As Carl Jung said, "There is no coming to consciousness without pain." That means that in most cases, people will choose to follow the road of blissful ignorance, rather than deal with the difficulty of incorporating new information into their thought process. The difficulty in breaking free of these subconscious blocks greatly depends on the amount of mental abuse that the individual has been subject to over the course of their lifetime. The reason for this is due to the toxic environment in which consciousness exists in, where most people are deliberately kept in their lowest state of energy to maintain the status quo here.

An example that I often like to use to help describe the various environments that exist for expanding one's awareness, is by picturing consciousness as a small sapling tree that's growing on the forest floor. Growth of the young tree is directly dependent on the amount of light and nourishment that it receives. The more conducive and beneficial that the environment is, the higher the chance that exponential growth will occur. On the other hand, the more darkness and shade that it gets, the more it will struggle to grow. That means that with the proper environment and stimuli in place, the expansion of consciousness can occur quite rapidly in some individuals. When one experiences this spiritual path of heightened awareness and energy, it can be a truly profound and humbling experience that can fundamentally alter a person's path in life.

Mysteries of Ancient History

Across the Earth, ancient ruins and megalithic structures such as Sacsayhuamán in Peru, the Temple of Jupiter in Lebanon, or Gobekli Tepe in Turkey have been proven to be far older than what our modern history books are willing to admit. In fact, the incredible megalithic site of Gobekli Tepe, located in the Southeastern Anatolia Region of Turkey, has been radiocarbon dated to be *over* 11,000 years old. Meanwhile, further to the west in Baalbek, Lebanon, the ancient city of Heliopolis and the Temple of Jupiter contain enormous stone blocks that are in excess of 1,000 tons each. Yet at the same time, most mainstream experts will tell you that these megalithic sites were built *less* than 5,000 years ago by the Romans, or some nomadic hunter-gatherer group, using nothing more than bronze-age tools. This evidence greatly contradicts what society has been taught about the timeline of human history and helps to paint a far different picture of our past.

The most important question is, why isn't this important information part of our education system? From the secret tunnels found beneath the pyramids of Giza and the water erosion marks on the Sphinx Enclosure, to the knowledge of mathematics and astronomy developed by the early Sumerians of Mesopotamia, around the world, we find compelling evidence that suggests that human civilizations are far older and more sophisticated than what we've been told.

This brings up serious questions as to *why* this important evidence still remains unknown to most of society. To answer that difficult question, we must objectively review this evidence, the nature of reality, and the secrets of ancient history.

For far too long, society has based their understanding of the events of the past and present upon a small number of "experts" in their field and rarely choose to question or seek alternative theories. This disastrous outcome, based on generations of misguided and docile trust, is the very reason why I'm writing these words to you now. This conclusion may be hard for some to accept, but the fact is plain and simple, we've been lied to for a *very* long time. The truth is far more fascinating to learn about than the biased and mundane version we've been given. Once the individual discovers the vast amount of evidence that exists which challenges the entire paradigm we've been taught, their perspective about the universe, history, science, and religion often changes forever. So now you may be wondering, what exactly have we been lied to about?

One of the most significant of these deceptions revolves around the incorrect information that's been provided by many of the mainstream archeologists about the true age and purpose of the pyramids of Giza, Egypt. We're told by many of these "experts" that the largest structures on Earth were built to honor the great pharaohs of Egypt. This lie is generally accepted by the majority of society, who is often too busy to take the time to research alternate theories for themselves. Yet today, not one pharaoh has *ever* been found in the pyramids of Giza, or in most of the other pyramids located around the world. The objective researcher quickly discovers that the

Egyptian pharaohs were buried more than 400 miles to the south, in a place called the Valley of the Kings. Famous pharaohs throughout history, such as Ramesses or Tutankhamun, were mummified and buried at the Valley of the Kings, surrounded by generations of older Dynastic Egyptian rulers.

So why have they deceived society about the truth and purpose of these pyramids? The answer to that question can be found by understanding the level of control that exists regarding the perception of history, which is fiercely guarded by powerful individuals and secret societies, who hide the true age and sophistication of many of these ancient civilizations. That means that even today, with all the modern technology that we have available to us, we would *still* have trouble constructing the pyramids of Egypt. The design and alignments of these pyramids suggest that these ancient builders knew detailed information about both mathematics and the constellations of our galaxy, as well as the electromagnetic energy and ratio of the Earth. If this information was released to the public, it would not only change our understanding of consciousness and energy but alter the entire way we view human history.

These spectacular achievements in engineering were only made possible because of a specific understanding of the precise ratio of the Earth, as well as the ley lines of energy that cross the planet. But how could they have known that more than 10,000 years ago? Evidence shows that the true purpose behind this intuitive design was to create a large structure that could focus and harness unlimited electromagnetic energy, as well as to act as a type of harmonic resonator to raise human consciousness. The real question is, what could they have needed all of this energy for thousands of years ago? To me, the obvious answer to that question suggests that these ancient civilizations were much more advanced than our history books are willing to admit.

In fact, not only are the pyramids of Giza far older than what we've been told, but the Dynastic pharaohs of Egypt were also *incorrectly* given credit for their creation. Evidence shows that these magnificent and precise structures were built by a lost civilization who disappeared from Earth's history during the last ice age. Furthermore, when looking at the positions of the constellations of Orion, Leo, and Canis Major 10,500-13,000 years ago, and accounting for the precessional changes that occur to the Earth, it can be fascinating to learn that both the Great Pyramid and Sphinx perfectly align to these star constellations during that time period. For those who don't know, axial precession is caused by the slight wobbling of an astronomical body, which causes its orientation to change over time. This creates what is known as the precession of the equinoxes, or Zodiac Ages, which represents a cycle of approximately 25,700 years.

This dating evidence also correlates strikingly well with the water erosion marks that have been found along the edges of the Sphinx Enclosure, which strongly suggests that the true age of these structures is far older than what we've been told based on the historical rainfall patterns for the region. Along with the deception given about the truth of the pyramids of Giza and the Sphinx, the Temple of Seti in the city of Abydos, Egypt provides even further evidence to show the advanced sophistication that these ancient civilizations achieved. What's so important about the Temple of Seti is that it contains unique hieroglyphs which clearly portray "modern vehicles", including a helicopter, a submarine, and a plane. But that's impossible right?

Cuneiform tablets from Mesopotamia, along with ice core samples from Greenland, and geologic evidence from across the world, strongly suggest that a series of devastating cataclysms occurred on the Earth between 10,500 and 12,800 years ago, leading to rapid melting of the ice caps, global floods, and destructive climate changes. These cataclysms were likely caused by a large solar outburst from the Sun, or possibly a comet strike, which wiped out many of the ancient civilizations that were present on the planet, causing their existence and memory to become nearly lost to time. A great deal of their knowledge and advanced technology was destroyed in these cataclysms, however, some of the megalithic structures and pyramids they built still remain today.

According to the famous philosopher Plato, a sophisticated civilization called Atlantis once existed somewhere south-west of the Straights of Gibraltar in western Africa, on a string of circular islands that formed a large central landmass. These writings, known as the Timaeus and Critias, state that Atlantis was destroyed by a series of violent catastrophes that were so severe that little remained of it afterward. This information provided by Plato, describing these cataclysms that occurred at the end of the last ice age, correlates strikingly well with Mesopotamian cuneiform tablets, ancient stories, biblical writings, and ice core data from Greenland, all of which provide a glimpse into what occurred long ago. These disasters led to the destruction of many of the Pre-Diluvian civilizations that once thrived on the planet. Yet little about this information is ever discussed on an academic level and is still largely considered pseudoarcheology by most mainstream experts.

It should become clear that we can no longer trust the antiquated view of history we've been given. Furthermore, the particular way that society perceives evolution, human origins, and their purpose in the universe, has been manipulated and conditioned for so long, that most have become unbalanced and ignorant of what the truth is. Throughout the course of this book, I will be going into extensive details to explain *how* exactly that was accomplished. Remember, the truth can be hard to stomach at times since it's been largely written by the victors, which often portrays a biased and false viewpoint that isn't supported by the evidence. This false perception of reality, along with the control of ancient history and consciousness, formed the basis for my previous book entitled, *The Illusion of Us: The Suppression and Evolution of Human Consciousness*.

This book promises to continue where that left off, delving much deeper than before to help answer some of our most difficult questions. However, before we go any further, it's important to develop an understanding of how to objectively view facts and information accurately to develop logical conclusions. This is a necessary step for any good researcher to take who's searching for the truth. The famous detective Arthur Conan Doyle gave a profound quote that should act as the means for building this foundation of reason. He said, "Once you eliminate the impossible, whatever remains, no matter how improbable, must be the truth." Let those words resonate deep within you and decide for yourself what's real and what's simply a clever distraction from the truth. The goal of this book is to help to establish a framework for better understanding the complexities of reality and the universe, as well as the secrets of the past and gods of history. Let's begin.

Energy, Dimensions, and the Universe

Since ancient times, certain individuals such as Hermes, Buddha, or Krishna have managed to reach such a heightened state, both physically and mentally, that they were able to transform their consciousness and energy into pure light. This allowed them to transcend beyond the limits of the third-dimensional world to master all of reality. That's why so many cultures across history have studied and worshipped these individuals and the teachings they left behind. For thousands of years, this knowledge has been carefully guarded and hidden within certain secret societies and elite families because of how powerful it is and what it can awaken in humanity.

The Egyptians realized the importance of transcending the physical world in order to progress along the path of enlightenment. They called this struggle Ka, which represents the soul trapped in the body that's constantly blinded by illusions and deception. But who would want to stop this path of human ascension? As you travel deeper and deeper down the rabbit hole of knowledge, following the evidence trail of history, you begin to realize that not all beings and entities in the universe necessarily want the conscious evolution of others. In fact, some of these more malevolent entities *could* even decide to physiologically control less developed species for the means of tricking them into freely giving up their energy and creative potential. That's why transcending to a higher state of consciousness by breaking free of the chains of the material world is so guarded here, due in part to the law of free will and the predation of basic human urges.

The human brain functions as a powerful organic computer, and like all computers, it can become infected with viruses that come in the form of polluting thoughts and negative associations. Those negative or false associations can build up over time within us, and greatly affect the growth of consciousness. The challenge becomes how to heal and cleanse the mind and body, to free it from the bondage of its accumulated burdens. To me, the great feat to accomplish in this life should not merely revolve around scaling the highest mountain or deepest canyon, but rather exploring the wonders and secrets within the human mind.

I often compare the process of an individual expanding their conscious awareness to the analogy of a dark forest that they must traverse. This dark forest contains many different pathways, each of them promising an easy way out of the darkness. Those who follow these easy paths often find out too late that they've been tricked and misled for not taking the more challenging route. Instead of an "easy" road to ascension, the path to reach higher states of consciousness and energy has been purposely made difficult, and any shortcuts taken are severely punished along the way. The real question is, who created this system? The answer to that difficult question will be thoroughly explained in subsequent chapters.

This journey of freeing the mind from the material world and becoming a higher conscious being is one of the hardest things you will ever do in your lifetime and should not be taken lightly. But for those on the serious path, who want to rise above and transcend to a higher reality of existence, these teachings may provide the means to assist you on your difficult journey. Remember, following along this dusty road of truth often takes great courage and sacrifice. However, the rewards can exceed anything that can be achieved in a lower state of energy and represent our true purpose here on Earth.

The first place to begin is to better understand the reality and universe that surrounds us. But is our universe really singular, or is it actually a multiverse? According to the laws of superstring theory and the knowledge handed down by ancient cultures, we're living in what's known as a multiverse, that's composed of countless different versions of reality that are all layered on top of one another. However, for the sake of ease, I will be primarily using the term universe throughout the rest of the book, even though it's not actually singular at all.

Going deeper, all of these different timelines that exist throughout the vast universe are being played out on the great stage of the physical, third-dimensional world, where they're separated by both higher and lower dimensions. The goal of this sandwich-like reality is to always strive to preserve balance, harmony, and the principles of free will. The laws of superstring theory explain that all matter can be reduced down to strings of vibrating energy, each with its own varying frequency. These countless strings of vibration are all connected and influenced through the properties of electromagnetism, which is derived from the mass of a physical object such as a planet or star. This creates the effect we refer to as gravity. That's how Nikola Tesla was able to generate free energy through the electromagnetic grid of the Earth since he discovered what the pyramid builders of antiquity had already learned.

Due to the nature of these principles that define the laws of the universe, a hierarchy system formed within these varying states of energy and matter, which are separated by at least nine different dimensions. The majority of these dimensions are non-physical, which means that most of what's occurring in them are invisible to our limited perceptions. This forms the basis for the important concept of "as above, so below", which is shown across nearly every ancient society of the past. As we incorporate these concepts into our mind, we often change as an individual, and suddenly view much of reality and consciousness in a different *light*.

While there exist both higher and lower dimensions, the third dimension is particularly important because it represents where matter and energy can take on physical form. That's a key point to understand and remember going forward. The Earth acts as either a school for exploring self-expression in a physical body or a prison that can trap consciousness behind a veil of illusions. It all depends on your perspective. If an individual decides to focus entirely on the material world, they'll likely have to return through the incarnation cycle to repeat the process again until they finally choose to grow on a spiritual level. This process of human ascension can take countless lifetimes to master and greatly depends on a variety of complex factors. I will be going into much greater detail regarding the fundamentals of dimensions later on. To fully understand how these conscious changes can profoundly alter the course of one's life, we must first understand what a timeline is.

A timeline is the linear measure of the events of the past which are categorized in chronological order. By not recognizing or understanding that each one of us plays a part in the overall timeline of humanity, most individuals care little about their actions or how they could affect others. At the same time, most of society is kept in the dark about the importance of spirituality and connecting to a higher level of conscious awareness. The consequences for this unbalanced and polluted mindset can be seen through the extreme division, war, and uneven distribution of resources across the entire planet, where both gluttony and severe malnourishment are prevalent at the same time.

This destructive mindset not only threatens the balance of life on Earth but the entire future of the human race from self-annihilation. When the truth finally comes out that we're not the only sentient beings that exist in the universe and are a part of something much greater than ourselves, it will force a great awakening to occur where most people will have to redefine how they perceive reality and consciousness. For many of us though, it feels like we've been patiently waiting for that moment for an eternity. Alan Watts once said, "You are an aperture through which the universe is looking at and exploring itself."

We should never forget that we're all playing a part in this collective story of humanity, where each one of us is contributing in some way towards the direction that our society will take. The choice of traveling down this difficult road of seeking truth and spreading wisdom is often called "the good work," and represents the courage found within one's soul to choose a path of light and knowledge. This decision means that the individual must take time to study and understand the nature of reality and consciousness so they can develop the necessary perspective to help others. The easiest way to start this process is by walking outside on a clear night, as far from light pollution as possible, and simply looking up.

Lying out on the grass at night beneath the twinkling starlight of countless distant stars and planets, scattered across a nearly infinite cosmos, I often wonder to myself, "who else is looking back?" To conclude that we're alone in the universe would be both silly and illogical based on our limited perspective, and the conscious mind would only have to look at the conclusions found in the important Drake equation to see the potential of all that may exist beyond our small vantage point here.

Try to fully comprehend the idea that we're located on one of the spiral bands of the Milky Way Galaxy, surrounded by billions of other star system and planets whose number is so inconceivably large, that if added up it would exceed every grain of sand on all the beaches of Earth. Allow that staggering number and sheer size to sink in. Soon you become a conscious observer who's aware of yourself and your place within the universe.

Considering the vast size of the cosmos and the overwhelming odds that advanced sentient lifeforms exist, you may be asking yourself, "where are they all?" This commonly asked question fits into what's known as the Fermi Paradox. The Fermi Paradox; named after physicist Enrico Fermi, points out the apparent contradiction between a lack of direct evidence for extraterrestrial civilizations, while at the same time factoring in the high probability that they do exist. Those probabilities are determined using the important Drake equation which I will be explaining in much greater detail throughout the course of the book. I would like to strongly point out that I do believe that compelling evidence can be found across the world that suggests that advanced beings or entities influenced ancient cultures long ago, however much of that evidence has been destroyed or suppressed within the general public. This has led to the false conclusion that we're all alone in the universe when really the answer is much more complicated.

The Drake equation, named after Frank Drake, states that the Earth is merely one of the *millions* of other possible planets that exist in the galaxy that could potentially support sentient life. That conclusion is based on an understanding of the necessary ingredients needed for supporting complex lifeforms, such as carbon and hydrogen, both of which are commonly found throughout the Milky Way Galaxy and beyond. Furthermore, the older the age of a star system, the more likely it is to harbor sentient beings, especially those planets which fall into what's known as the Goldilocks Zone.

The term "Goldilocks Zone" means that the necessary environmental and atmospheric conditions needed to support life would be present on the surface of any planetary bodies, which are found within a certain proximity to their nearest star. This, of course, is highly dependent on the prevalence of comet and asteroid strikes, as well as other complex factors, such as solar outbursts and destructive seismic activity, which could greatly affect the outcome of a planet.

The Drake equation postulates that there are potentially millions of planets in our Milky Way Galaxy alone where sentient life could have developed over the course of billions of years. Instead of the perception that we're all alone in the universe, we must accept the fact that life likely exists nearly *everywhere*. This is especially true when factoring in the effects of any hydrothermal vents or internal heating that may be present on some planetary bodies which appear to be too cold at first glance. These important conclusions mean that there's likely a nearly infinite number of Earth-like worlds that exist in the cosmos and we should collectively accept this mindset, rather than allowing the cynical perspective we've been given to cloud our awareness and judgment.

Using objective logic, it stands to reason that *most* intelligent extraterrestrial civilizations who developed the capability to leave their star system would likely try to remain invisible to the perceptions of any less developed species they encountered to not pollute their timeline. However, based on the history of Earth this may not always be the case. The reason for this is primarily due to two factors, such as the limitations of human perceptions, as well as the ability for some of these beings/entities to potentially exist and move between different dimensions. Instead of the concept of lifeforms developing independently on different worlds, beginning in primordial pools of sludge and later evolving to become highly conscious beings, we should expand our thinking to include outside influences and the theories of panspermia.

Due to this hierarchical system that exists in the cosmos, its likely allowed certain beings or entities throughout history to take on the persona of "gods" to those civilizations they encountered that are less developed than them. At times these visitors may have promoted great leaps in consciousness and technology, while at other times their influences could have given rise to warring empires and turmoil. Some of these beings and entities, sometimes referred to as fallen angels or demons in certain religions across the world, could have secretly manipulated mankind from the shadows for centuries without their awareness. Evidence shows that the reason for this is because these beings may have become so advanced, that they managed to transcend beyond the physical realm, allowing them to exist in both higher and lower dimensions.

Cuneiform tablets explain that these advanced beings, sometimes referred to as the Anunna in the Atrahasis, Anunnaki in the Enuma Elish, or the Children of Light in the Emerald Tablets, may have played a major role in the history of mankind, possibly even incarnating into our reality as a human at certain times. As difficult as that may be for many to accept, allow me to explain further and provide evidence to back up this statement.

Over the course of thousands of years, most of the Mesopotamian cuneiform tablets and ancient texts from the past that described these "gods" were either destroyed by cataclysms or invading armies, turning their memory and influence into nothing more than a myth. Many of these ancient texts that managed to survive were eventually re-written and used within some of the Abrahamic religions of the world. This created great confusion for generations over what the truth really was, while at the same time allowing those in power to continuously rule through the use of fear and ignorance.

This hidden hand of control, along with an antiquated and biased education system taught to the population, led to much of our history becoming greatly misunderstood and nearly lost. One of the most effective means of breaking out of this conditioned mentality is to realize that our eternal-conscious energy exists beyond the limitations of the third dimension and that each of us is having a physical experience in a mortal human body.

The real question is, what is the truth about the past and why would it be hidden from society in the first place? Before we answer that, we must first define what awareness is and how it plays an important role in achieving higher states of consciousness, as well as understanding the nature of reality. The term awareness can be defined by one's ability to recognize the larger picture that surrounds them, through the means of increasing their knowledge base and expanding their perceptions. You may be wondering why learning this information would be considered so crucial in your daily life that you would want to spend your precious time and energy to understand it? The reason may startle or even captivate many who read these words, for the secrets of ancient history provide compelling evidence to help answer many of our most important questions, as well as how we perceive our purpose in the universe.

There will undoubtedly be some who read these words that will immediately reject this information as impossible. However, if the individual has the courage to reach all the way to the end of the book, objectively considering all the evidence and conclusions presented, then much of this may make logical sense and could even provide the necessary spark needed to forge a new way of thinking. The important wisdom and knowledge that was imparted by ancient civilizations and secret societies of history can become an effective tool for the expansion of consciousness if in the right hands. In fact, merely reading these words could alter your entire life. That's not meant to be an egotistical statement, but rather one that's based on direct experience studying these ancient civilizations and understanding *why* they fought so hard to protect what I'm about to tell you.

Many of the groups who've historically protected this knowledge, such as the Druids or Gnostics, became systematically targeted and hunted down for eradication by those who didn't want this information to *ever* come out. The reason the truth is so protected and hidden from most of society is due to the sheer power that this information has on expanding human consciousness and altering one's perspective. My primary goal with this book is to expand upon the evidence and logical conclusions left behind from the sacrifice of countless researchers and gifted minds who came before me, who collectively have helped to resurrect this important knowledge so that it can finally be known once again. I seek to objectively understand what the larger truth is behind our reality, no matter where that road leads.

I can't overstate the importance of studying a multitude of different esoteric texts and teachings from across the world to better understand consciousness, energy cycles, the universe, and even the origins of mankind. The most significant of these writings include the cuneiform tablets from Mesopotamia, Sanskrit, Egyptian and Gnostic texts, and the ancient knowledge protected by the Maya and Aztec cultures. Due to the degradation of information over time, along with suppression and tampering, significant confusion developed over the events of ancient history. The analogy of the game "telephone" perfectly illustrates this point.

In the children's game of telephone, information is passed around and shared with each person in the circle.

The original message becomes more and more degraded over time. In order to find the purest form of truth, you must always seek the source of where that information came from. This means that cuneiform tablets such as the Sumerian King List, Atrahasis, Eridu Genesis, and Enuma Elish, represent some of the most unbiased and accurate ways to understand our history since they're some of the oldest texts ever written. These writings should be held in the highest regard as long as the individual always uses the most accurate translations available.

The reason that studying and understanding these texts is so important is that they contain the accumulated wisdom from thousands of years of history. If one tries to skip this step, they'll likely never be able to fully comprehend the sheer scope and complexity of our reality. Remember, knowledge is the main building block towards achieving higher states of consciousness and balance. Many of the cultures from the past, such as the Egyptians, Sumerians, or Maya, realized the importance of knowledge in their society and created large monuments and temples to honor it. These ancient civilizations left behind megalithic structures which were precisely aligned to worship the Sun, seasonal cycles, or specific star constellations during the precession of the equinoxes. This provides credible evidence to show the advanced sophistication they had achieved more than 10,000 years ago, long before the history books are willing to admit.

The serpent god Kukulkan taught the Maya that human consciousness followed various cycles which were based on several factors, including the particular level of vibrational energy present on the Earth, Zodiac Ages, and the position of the Solar System within the Milky Way Galaxy. This knowledge is portrayed particularly well in the Mayan city of Chichen Itza, with the specific design seen with the step pyramid known as Kukulkan's Temple, shown below in Figure 1.

Figure 1

Each of the nine levels of Kukulkan's Temple represents the nine different stages of human consciousness, with the top representing universal consciousness. Kukulkan was known as the feathered serpent-dragon god of the Maya, who gave them wisdom and knowledge from the heavens, as well as how to obtain balance and harmony with the Earth. The term "plumed" or "feathered" represents the transformation of the serpent into its highest state of energy, known as the dragon, much in the same way that the medical caduceus symbol represents the ascension of human energy to reach Kundalini. One of the other important reasons why the symbol of the serpent has been used so often in the past is due to the fact that the snake frequently sheds its skin to take on a new form, which represents the internal changes that occur within us when we unlock our chakra centers of energy to obtain higher states of consciousness. It's important to understand and differentiate the lies and deceit that have been perpetrated on society for centuries regarding the symbols of the eagle and serpent. That's why I will be spending a considerable amount of time in this book explaining the truth behind what they really represent and their significance in the rise and fall of human civilizations throughout history.

The Maya believed that the year 2012 would herald the conclusion of a great cycle of energy on Earth and in the cosmos and that instead of representing the apocalypse and the end of the world, it represented the rebirth after the death of what's known as "the old reality" that once existed here. The most important thing to understand about both the Maya and Aztec is that they eventually became corrupted through the practice of blood sacrifice and war, long before Cortés arrived. I will be extensively covering this area later on in the book, but I wanted to bring this topic up early in order to clarify some misconceptions that still exist surrounding these civilizations.

The destructive and lower vibrational acts of blood sacrifice and war seen in the Maya and Aztec cultures do not originate from either of the serpent-dragon gods of Kukulkan or Quetzalcoatl, both of who clearly state in ancient texts that they're firmly against these practices. In fact, both of these serpent-dragon gods of the Maya and

Aztec are closely related and based on similar influences. One of the main reasons why this book will focus so heavily on eagle and serpent symbolism is due to how extensively it can be found in cultures all across the world. From North and South America, all the way across the Atlantic Ocean to Egypt, Mesopotamia, India, and Japan, these important symbols have played a major role in many of the ancient civilizations of antiquity.

Symbolism and Duality

On a somewhat linear level, the eagle and serpent can be equated to masculine strength and control over the physical world, versus following a path of spiritual growth and obtaining higher knowledge. However, these symbols have much deeper meanings that can be traced back to some of the earliest texts ever written. In many ways, the eagle and serpent represent the divide that exists between the material third-dimensional world and the non-physical spiritual realms. Considering that humans are multidimensional beings, these two symbols represent the eternal struggle of which path our species will take in the future-either one ruled through military conquest and control, or higher knowledge and balance. However, as I have previously stated, these symbols are *not* merely just a way to show human archetypes and self-expression but can be connected all the way back to the early influences of the Anunna, who played the role of gods to mankind.

Over the course of this book, I will be providing extensive evidence to show the influences of the eagle and serpent throughout human history, including the

Maya, Aztec, and Inca cultures, all the way to the Roman, Greek, German, Russian, and Spanish Empires. In each of these examples, the various "gods" represented through the symbol of the eagle and phoenix managed to take over and corrupt the serpent-dragon cultures that were once present on the planet, until over time, only fragments of their wisdom and teachings remained. You will hear me bring up this point of corruption by the eagle many times throughout the course of this book as it's a very important concept to understand. This war, or struggle of the eagle and serpent, forms the basis for what we think of as *duality* in our reality.

Strewn across the world, remnants of this great legacy left behind from the serpent-dragon gods can still be seen in statues and temples from ancient Egypt, all the way to Mesoamerica and India, showing the positive influences these wisdom bringers had on these ancient cultures. Even in Greek mythology, the god Poseidon with his three-pronged trident is frequently connected to the symbol of the serpent, while his counterpart Zeus is connected with the symbol of the eagle. Both of these Greek gods were likely incarnations, or personas, of the earlier Mesopotamian gods played by Enki and Enlil.

Evidence for this can be seen in the various depictions and statues of Enki, which clearly portray him holding a trident, one of his most cherished symbols. That's why it's so fascinating to discover that the religious entity known as Satan or the Devil is almost always shown as an evil being from "hell" who's wielding a pitchfork. But was he really evil or is there more to the story? An objective analysis of the evidence reveals that the pitchfork is clearly the *inversion* of Enki and his trident, representing the role he eventually took on in the underworld. This clever perversion of the facts, perpetrated by certain Abrahamic religions and secret societies of the world, was done as a means to demonize his positive influences and teachings from the past.

Following this evidence trail around the planet allows a nearly forgotten story of history to emerge and finally be told. Any time that a serpent or dragon is portrayed in artwork or in an edifice (meaning large building,) it means that at *one* point that civilization was based on the acquisition of knowledge and obtaining higher states of consciousness. One of the best examples of this can be seen at the base of Kukulkan's Temple, shown below in Figure 2, where serpent-dragon statues guard the path of human ascension.

Figure 2

Physical Reality and Consciousness

On a vibrational and molecular level, the human body should be viewed as an organic vessel for consciousness to experience a physical reality in the third dimension. This physical body is primarily composed of water which contains electrical impulses that flow through the nerves and along the spinal cord. These electrical impulses function as a type of super antenna, allowing the brain to connect to higher states of energy and consciousness. Imagine your eternal soul energy as a signal on a radio station which is tuning in from across another dimension. That antenna can only operate correctly if it exists in a certain state of good health and vibration.

The unhealthier and more disconnected a person gets from their true selves and the natural world around them, the more their antenna will become disrupted and could even cease to function properly. When one objectively looks at the state of our reality, they quickly see a world full of negative stimuli and illusion, aimed at keeping people conformed and in a lower state of energy. This creates a clever "trap" which prevents most of society from achieving higher states of consciousness.

Due to the accumulation of toxins and heavy metals in the body over time, such as fluoride, aluminum, and mercury, the pineal gland in the brain, known as the third eye, becomes calcified in most individuals which renders it inactive. To achieve higher states of consciousness you must first cleanse these toxins from the body to activate this important gland, as well as becoming grounded to the energy of the Earth. In a way, human beings represent a type of organic battery that heavily relies on a balanced system to function at peak efficiency.

The Egyptian pharaohs and priests of antiquity knew the importance of activating the pineal gland in order to reach these higher states of conscious awareness and used the symbol of the serpent on the forehead to represent this transformation. In fact, this same symbol was also used in many ancient Hindu-Indian cultures, where it was portrayed through the coiled snake of the Kundalini. That's why the information contained in the Vedic texts can overlap so much with Egyptian and Mesopotamian teachings since they all had common influences. It's important to understand that the evolution of human consciousness is part of a great cycle that exists throughout the Solar System and universe, represented through the various states of energy which are constantly in a state of change. Remember, energy can never be created or destroyed, it can only change state.

If these ancient teachings are followed correctly for raising one's awareness and achieving spiritual balance, the seven energy chakra centers of the body, perfectly tuned with the seven colors of the visible light spectrum, begin to activate and allow the great metamorphosis of the body, mind, and spirit to take place. This was the original purpose and meaning behind the famous symbol of the cross and Trinity, representing the *crossing* of energy to reach Kundalini. The origins of these symbols can be traced all the way back to early Mesopotamia with what was known as the "Old Religion", before eventually becoming associated with Christianity and the Holy Roman Empire. The true meanings behind these important symbols have become nearly lost to history, much in the same way that the swastika was.

This forbidden secret behind reaching what became known as "Christ consciousness" or Kundalini, has been suppressed for thousands of years by powerful religious groups and certain secret societies, who have conditioned most of the public to follow a deceitful and greatly watered-down version of the truth. That's why it's so important that one understands the fundamentals of energy, consciousness, and vibration, to comprehend the significance of the different chakra centers of the body and their relationship to the visible light spectrum. The fact that our chakra centers just so happen to perfectly reflect and match the visible light spectrum is further evidence to show that genetic tampering of our DNA occurred in the distant past. To me, it would be extremely difficult to account for these anomalies using the standard Darwinian model of evolution.

Now you may be wondering how exactly we ended up in a reality based on suppression, war, and deceit? Before I continue any further into our ancient past, I want to provide a profound quote from Barbara Marciniak, which perfectly describes the illusion that has enslaved and blocked off the truths of our reality. I have used this quote in my previous book, but I feel it's necessary to share again to understand the larger picture that surrounds us. Carefully read and reflect on the following words: "The ultimate tyranny in a society is not control by martial law, but control by the psychological manipulation of consciousness, through which reality is defined so that those who exist within it, do not even realize they are in prison."

When we're born, we awaken into a world based on a certain generational understanding of how to perceive reality that has been passed down by our parents. In most cases, they only acquired this perspective from what *they* were told from so-called "experts" and authoritarian figures, which caused most to follow a greatly biased and antiquated viewpoint of history, spirituality, and the nature of reality. This created the version of reality that we exist in today, where we're taught that our true purpose here is to simply acquire financial success and material gain by sacrificing most of our time and energy.

Eventually, this farm of conformity and mental conditioning led to tremendous unbalance throughout most of society, giving rise to generations of zombie-like people who do very little critical thinking and mainly focus on empty pleasures to get through each day. At the same time, powerful secret societies and corrupted governments continue to promote this false doctrine to maintain the status quo. The famous book, *1984* by George Orwell, provides some shockingly accurate viewpoints that perfectly describes this Orwellian-like world that's been created here. We must collectively stand together and realize the dangerous direction we're all headed in, through the means of ignorance, materialism, and hate, and instead forge our own path to see through the empty illusions which have blinded us for so long.

Unfortunately, most people never ask the question of where exactly these rules and laws forming the basis of our reality came from. The incorrect assumption to make is that everything we see is simply based on the natural course of human history and Darwinian evolution. This has created the misconception that human beings are nothing more than an evolved ape and that all the war and chaos on the planet is caused by us struggling to overcome our primitive nature. This greatly antiquated and incorrect theory to explain our origins and purpose will be brought up multiple times throughout the course of this book, as it's one of the major reasons why mankind has been held back for so long.

To some, this may seem impossible and nothing more than a bunch of wild conspiracy theories; while to others, it could help to connect and answer many of our most important questions. This is due to the particular level of conscious awareness that each of us has obtained over the course of our lifetime and whether or not we're able to objectively consider and incorporate this information into our thought process. Remember, if these concepts can't be connected and understood on a higher level, they'll likely be rejected by the individual due to their complexity. To fully understand this "bigger picture", continue on with me to the next chapter, where I extensively discuss the important events of ancient history and explain the origins of where religion, laws, agriculture, and the entire structure to our reality came from.

(1,2,10,11,13,14,19,20)

CHAPTER 2

LOST HISTORY AND ANCIENT ORIGINS

In this chapter, I'm going to be presenting you with concepts that may challenge everything you think you know about science, history, and even the origins of mankind. This information is based on studying the evidence from around the world within cuneiform tablets and sacred texts, to ice core samples and megalithic structures, all of which help to fill in important gaps in understanding our past. The most critical concept that is echoed across nearly every one of these ancient cultures explains that as a human, you have the potential within yourself to fundamentally alter all of reality, becoming spiritually and consciously aware of your higher purpose in the universe. This is the overall reason why we've seen so much war, persecution, and division throughout history since *some* feel threatened of what the human race could collectively become in the future. As difficult as that concept may be to accept right now, allow me to present evidence that supports these claims.

With so many lies constantly bombarding society from nearly all directions, it can be very difficult to separate what the truth really is from all the misinformation and deception that plagues us. One of the keys to achieving this lofty goal is to objectively study ancient history to understand the origins of where science, mathematics, philosophy, laws, astronomy, and agriculture all came from. To do that, we must travel back to one of the earliest civilizations on Earth known as the Sumerians.

According to some of mankind's oldest historical records, the origins of complex laws, mathematics, agriculture, astronomy, and even currency began with the Sumerians of Mesopotamia, less than 6,000 years ago. However, I would like to point out that there is extensive evidence that can be found which *strongly* supports the hypothesis that much older human civilizations existed in this region more than 12,000 years ago, during the time period known as the Pleistocene Epoch. Unfortunately, most of those ancient records were lost over time, but not *all* of them. I will be going into much more detail about these Pre-Diluvian civilizations later in the chapter.

The Sumerians claimed that all the knowledge they had acquired was handed down to them from *gods* who resided above them in *heaven*. This concept of "heaven" can best be equated to the higher dimensions and anything beyond the physical realm of Earth, while "hell" refers to the underworld and lower dimensions. One of the best pieces of evidence that supports these claims is the Sumerian King List, which is a cuneiform tablet from Mesopotamia that lists out the long reigns of many of its early rulers, as well as where kingship, laws, and early agriculture came from. The opening statement in the Sumerian King List says, "When kingship was lowered from heaven, kingship was in Eridu."

Both the Sumerian King List and Eridu Genesis tablets claim that Eridu was the first city on Earth where kingship was lowered to. These cuneiform tablets discuss these cities in detail, as well as the kings who were *chosen* to rule there.

The Eridu Genesis tablet states:

"When the royal scepter was coming down from heaven, the august crown and the royal throne being already down from heaven, the king regularly performed to perfection the august divine services and offices, and laid the bricks of those cities in pure spots.

The firstling of the cities, Eridu, she gave to the leader Nudimmud, the second, Bad-Tibira, she gave to the Prince and the Sacred One, the third, Larak, she gave to Pahilsag, the fourth, Sippar, she gave to the gallant Utu, the fifth, Suruppak, she gave to Ansud."

The reason that these Mesopotamian cuneiform tablets are so important is that the information they contain correlates remarkably well together, which helps to support their authenticity. These early texts completely rewrite the false narrative that we've been taught in school, especially regarding mankind's early achievements and timeline. Most of what we see today is the direct result of these influences that occurred long ago. To see the truth more clearly, we should rid ourselves of our foolish pride and instead only follow the evidence and facts.

Money, Conspiracies, and the Central Bank

Records indicate that the Sumerians of Mesopotamia were among the first people to utilize a form of currency for commerce. They called this form of currency a "shekel" which represented a two-sided coin that had a value equal to a bushel of wheat. This evidence not only helps to explain where the first form of currency came from but also shows how important agriculture was to their society. In fact, if you break down the name shekel, the word "she" meant wheat, and "kel" meant the measurement of a single bushel. What's so significant to understand about a shekel is that its value was entirely based on the specific measurement of a necessary commodity in the community, which in this case was wheat. Think about what that means for a moment when comparing the actual value of money in our current society today.

If a nation's currency is not backed by something with actual value, then it becomes unstable and extremely prone to manipulation and collapse. Looking all around the world at the numerous wars and conflicts being fought near large oil reserves, opium fields, and rare mineral deposits, it's clear that there's a mad race by some powerful industrialized countries to secure these important resources for themselves. However, despite this, evidence shows that most empires eventually collapse over time, due to their unsustainable nature.

The philosopher George Santayana gave a famous quote to explain this progressive ignorance when he said: "Those who do not learn history are destined to repeat it." Remember those words as we continue further into the book. This unfortunate outcome is one of the main reasons why money became such an integral part of our society, putting productivity above all else, even at the cost of creativity and self-expression. Once the focus of a population becomes structured purely around material gain and the accumulation of wealth, it becomes prone to immense greed, unbalance, and war. It should become apparent that our society; through generations of subconscious conditioning, has become greatly poisoned by this destructive mindset.

Today, this greedy and unsustainable governing structure has managed to corrupt and take over nearly everything in our reality, as most of the wealth of a nation is funneled to the very top through massive corporations and large banks. That means that any government whose finances are run by the privately owned and powerful Central Bank is often used as nothing more than puppets for a specific agenda. Sadly, this includes *most* of the industrialized nations of the world. One of the best examples of this can be seen with the United States through the privately-owned Federal Reserve, which is owned and operated by the Central Bank. So the real question is, who owns and runs the Central Bank?

It may be shocking for some to learn that the Central Bank is owned by one single family known as the

Rothschilds, who also determines the daily price of gold. Researching and studying the Rothschild family legacy is one of the keys to understanding how our reality became structured the way that it did. A profound quote which perfectly illustrates how this elite family was able to take over most of the governments of the world was made by James A. Garfield where he says, "He who controls the money supply of a nation controls the nation." That's why it's so fascinating to discover that the origins of the Rothschild family bloodline; along with many other elite families, can be traced all the way back to the early Sumerian and Babylonian kings of Mesopotamia. This is by no means a coincidence and provides clues to help explain how this ancient model of kingship came to define so much of our lives.

The Rothschild family dynasty was able to achieve supremacy through a clever two-pronged approach; first by seizing control of the global monetary systems, followed by the direct funding of certain empires and armed conflicts around the world. Remember, wars take a tremendous amount of resources and finances for a nation to wage, and in the end somebody *always* has to pay for them. One of the most difficult realizations to accept is that this secretive and powerful family dynasty has been responsible for the direct funding and even *creation* of many of the wars that have occurred over the last several hundred years. As difficult as that may be to accept, allow me to explain further. This destructive and devious mentality became collectively known as "the military industrial complex" in which several US presidents, such as Eisenhower and JFK, have repeatedly warned us about. Seems impossible right?

There is concrete evidence to support this "theory"

which goes far beyond what some would only call circumstantial. That evidence comes directly from Gutle Rothschild, who was the mother of the five most influential Rothschild banking sons in history. Shortly before she died Gutle nonchalantly stated, "If my sons did not want wars, there would be **none**." This uncomfortable quote means that *many* of the events that have led to wars in the past are in fact carefully calculated and planned. This perspective greatly differs with the viewpoint that's held by most of society, who are falsely conditioned into believing that these events are nothing more than the natural course of history. Realizations like these are why many people decide to ignore the truth and look the other way due to how difficult it can be to accept.

To give a little background first, Mayer Amschel Rothschild was considered to be the founder of the Rothschild banking dynasty, which emerged in Europe in the early 1800s. Mayer Amschel Rothschild was proceeded by his five sons, who he taught the art of currency exchange and foreign trade thanks to the skills he learned from Jacob Wolf Oppenheimer at his banking firm in 1758. The family name of "Oppenheimer" should be familiar to many considering that J. Robert Oppenheimer is credited as being the "father of the atomic bomb" during its development in the Manhattan Project, which was unveiled in Bohemian Grove. More about that later though. This is by no means a coincidence since each one of these men were part of certain secret societies whose influences would eventually give rise to the powerful global elites who control most of society today.

The five sons of Mayer Amschel Rothschild were

then strategically sent to the financial capitals of England, Italy, Germany, France, and Austria in order to establish independent branches there to represent the family's interests. Each of these important European countries was chosen based on the influences they had over the rest of the region. The Rothschilds knew that the key to controlling a country's affairs is directly through the ownership of its banking sector. Mayer Amschel Rothschild himself provides proof for this global monetary conspiracy when he famously stated: "Give me control of a nation's money and I care not who makes its laws."

Through the Central Bank, the Rothschild family dynasty was able to amass nearly unimaginable wealth; in excess of hundreds of trillions of dollars, which they used as leverage to govern other nations' interests. Once the Central Bank was established as the official bank of most of the industrialized countries around the world, it's power and influence was able to spread to nearly every corner of the planet, controlling not only finances, but politics, laws, and even education. Remember, these are not just empty conspiracy theories, but the real facts behind our history.

In order to understand all this more clearly and see the origins of where this kingship-governing structure came from, we should go back and objectively look at the events of ancient history. The model of kingship that has been ruling past civilizations for thousands of years represents the hierarchy pyramid design for society, where the true power and control lies within a small number of individuals at the very top. This can be clearly seen on the back of the one-dollar bill with the all-seeing eye, known as the Eye of Providence, and the unfinished pyramid. Those selected "rulers" at the top of the pyramid govern over the rest of the population and falsely condition them into believing that their governments made decisions based on their best interests. In reality, most of these governments are heavily controlled and monitored, and officials are kept in a state of strict obedience through the use of bribery, tariffs, blackmail, or even war for those who don't follow the rules.

A good example of this can be seen today with the war and instability that's rampant across the Middle East. It can be fascinating to learn that the war-torn nations of Libya, Iraq, Iran, and Syria are some of the only countries left which are *not* part of the Central Bank. One can't help but find that to be a little bit interesting and far more than simply a coincidence. Instead of this shocking realization being known by most of the public, the use of propaganda, artificially planted evidence, and paid militants have created the illusion that there's a common threat that we *all* must unite against. This tactic is often called a "false flag event" and is done to further an agenda or to fuel a war.

Those who follow and don't question the rules often achieve great financial success for their blind loyalty. Since the majority of society is still largely unaware of this information, or chooses to ignore it, most freely give up their time and energy towards seeking a certain level of comfort, regardless of what the real costs are associated with that. This mentality has created both large scale environmental destruction, as well as massive inequality and unbalance across nearly the entire planet. Someday in the future, this realization will finally be understood by the public, and we must collectively do everything in our power to prevent this atrocity from ever happening again.

The underlying reason why these global elites favor the suppression of consciousness, rather than its expansion, is due to several complex factors. These include a long-standing desire to maintain order and productivity within society, as well as hiding the identity of those who really govern over the rest of the world. I will be going into much more detail about what that means in the next several chapters. The researcher David Icke spoke about this hidden truth when he eloquently said, "When you look in the mirror, what do you see? Do you see the real you, or what you have been conditioned to believe is you? The two are so different. One is an infinite consciousness capable of being and creating whatever it chooses, the other is an illusion imprisoned by its own perceived and programmed limitations."

Generation after generation, the collective subconscious of society has been conditioned to attack any concepts or ideas that don't fit into the specific timeline and model of history that's been designated. Past cultures such as the Maya and Egyptians, frequently discussed this false paradigm in many of their ancient writings and sacred texts. They realized that mankind lived in a created veil of illusion based on our limited perception and lack of understanding of the universe that surrounds us. This lack of awareness caused humans to become eternally trapped in the physical world until they could finally grow consciously to realize their true nature. To better understand how the structure of society became so driven by its basic urges, we must first take a step back in order to see the bigger picture behind the fundamental principles that govern all of reality.

War of the Gods and the Rulers of Reality

Somewhat hypothetically speaking, since there are both higher and lower dimensions to reality, any advanced beings or entities that managed to transcend beyond the limits of the physical world could potentially influence or even control any sentient lifeforms that exist in less aware states below them. In most cases, this would likely occur without them *ever* knowing about it. That's one of the main reasons why the universe is perceived by many as being empty, since our collective consciousness hasn't reached the point yet where we're mature enough to know the truth.

Due to these hierarchy rules of awareness that exist, it means that any of these beings or entities that potentially influenced mankind's past would have remained largely hidden from the masses since they primarily communicated with enlightened priests and sages, as well as those in the upper echelons of society. That's how their legacy in the past became largely considered a myth since only those at the very top were privy to that knowledge. Over time though, those influences became less and less. But are these beings or entities in other dimensions real, and how have they influenced human history?

As hard as it may be to accept, our world is controlled by a very small number of extremely powerful people who are collectively known as the Global Elite, Illuminati, or Cabal. The purpose of this elite group of individuals may be to act as a type of delegate to represent the interests of some of these beings or entities who *still* maintain control of our reality today. As mind-boggling as that is to consider, I will be providing extensive evidence that supports these claims over the course of the book. In essence, this secret society maintains the kingship structure model here, in return for nearly unlimited power and wealth. After all, the puppet master doesn't reveal themselves to the audience until after the show is over. To better understand who these hidden rulers are, we must study the evidence from ancient history, which describes in great detail those who have been referred to as spirits, gods, genies, angels or demons.

There have been many names used throughout history to describe these beings: known as the Anunnaki to the Sumerians, the Jinn in Arabian mythology, the Elohim in the Hebrew Bible, the Watchers in the Book of Enoch, the Archons to the Gnostics, the Titans and Olympians to the Greeks, the Asuras and Devas in Hindu mythology, and countless others. No matter what you call them, the traits shared by these beings can be found in cultures across the world, and is impossible to ignore any longer. It's by no means a coincidence then that the word *Jinn* in Arabic means, "to hide," or "to conceal," while the word *Archon* in Gnosticism means "ruler."

In fact, going even a step further, the Gnostics not only referred to these beings and entities as "rulers" in the Nag Hammadi Scriptures, but more specifically the "rulers of reality." The Gnostics go on to explain that these beings remain hidden and nearly invisible to human perceptions by existing primarily in higher and lower dimensions where they can create chaos or provide knowledge to mankind at different time periods. Let's go further.

According to Mesopotamian cuneiform tablets, hundreds of thousands of years ago a group of advanced beings known as the Anunna, or Anunnaki came to the realm of Earth and conquered its reality, disrupting the balance and harmony that once existed. A decision was made by some of the Anunnaki to jumpstart the evolution of the early hominids found on Earth to create primitive workers that they could rule over. However, some of these beings ended up falling in love with their creation and secretly endowed Homo sapiens with their genetic gifts and the ability to reach higher states of consciousness. This was done in the hopes that humans could one day discover their true identity and eventually reach their full potential.

Due to this decision, many of these beings became greatly divided and continuously fought amongst one another over whether these gifts given to the human race were ever justified, as many of them felt we never deserved them in the first place. Because of this dualistic viewpoint, some of these beings put forth extensive effort to suppress or even permanently extinguish this spark of creation from within us. Many of the secret societies and mystery schools of the past knew that if mankind could ever manage to collectively raise their energy and conscious levels high enough, that they would eventually activate this dormant DNA to reach a new stage of their evolution. That's why certain texts and key pieces of information from history were guarded and protected, to ensure a path for future generations to follow.

The word Anunnaki translates to mean, "those who Anu sent from heaven to Earth," or "those who from heaven to Earth came." Unfortunately, this name has developed somewhat of a stigma over the years in much of the academic community and within social media, where many falsely believe the Anunnaki are simply a creation of Zechariah Sitchin and nothing more than a mistranslation. This has prevented a great deal of this important historical information from being known by most of the population and represents a dangerous precedent where facts and evidence are blindly ignored due to a lack of individual research and objective reasoning.

That's why I will be providing compelling evidence in this book to not only show that the Anunnaki are real, but that they have been extensively mentioned in translations by experts such as George Smith in his 1846 book: *The Chaldea Account of Genesis*, which was written over 50 years before Zechariah Sitchin. In fact, Stephany Dalley, another expert Assyriologist and researcher, verified the earlier work done by George Smith when she translated the Atrahasis cuneiform tablets. The point that I'm trying to get across here is that the name "Anunnaki" is not a creation from one man but represents one of the most important *keys* to the puzzle to accurately understand the past.

The phrases "heaven" and "hell" that are frequently found within many ancient writings and religious texts have been greatly misunderstood in society for generations. This is largely due to the polluted association that were given to them by certain Abrahamic religions, who often used them as a form of deceptive control. If you study these terms, you find that the word "heaven" simply meant from beyond the physical realm of Earth and the higher dimensions, while "hell" meant the underworld and lower dimensions. That's why some of these beings were called fallen angels in Biblical texts since they attempted to play God here and were cast down for eternity.

As difficult as it may be to wrap your head around, evidence shows that the Anunnaki are part of a superior group of beings or entities that are *far* older than humans. Some of them became so advanced that they eventually developed the ability to exist in non-corporeal form, as non-physical beings that can move between the higher and lower dimensions. This allowed them to influence our reality at any time using humans as hosts, or even physically incarnating here. That's the reason why we find so many different names and incarnations from them throughout history, and why Thoth mentions their presence in the Emerald Tablets as "hiding in the shadows" among mankind. You may be wondering, what evidence exists to support these claims?

One of the best pieces of evidence we have comes from the Mesopotamian cuneiform tablets known as the Atrahasis, where on tablet number two it states: "undue the chain and set us free." This phrase may seem simple at first; however, I feel that its deeper meaning can provide clues to some of the most complicated and misunderstood aspects of our reality. The term "chain" is referencing the hold that the third dimension has on a physical being, in which the Anunnaki sought to conquer and eventually did, becoming non-corporeal and having the ability to exist on an interdimensional level. That's why the Atrahasis explains that humans were *specifically* created to fulfill this particular role in the physical realm for them since the Igigi had revolted and refused to do it any longer.

Since the Anunnaki no longer had to be present in physical form here, only the most enlightened priests and mystics became permitted to contact them through altered states of consciousness and within certain rituals.

After catastrophes destroyed most of these advanced civilizations during the Younger Dryas period, the connections to these higher beings became less and less, until eventually they were considered by most to be merely a myth. This was largely because many of the temples and pyramids used by these sages and priests were destroyed or severely damaged by these disasters, and the legacy of wisdom being passed down to their descendants had substantially decreased over time.

Eventually, this absence of knowledge created a great spiritual divide within mankind, which resulted in many of the early Gnostic and Mesopotamian texts to be tampered with and re-written to personify these beings as angels, demons, and gods within religion. This caused a significant amount of information to become hidden within clever allegories and religious teachings, where their true meanings became *nearly* lost. That's how a greatly antiquated version of history became taught to much of society. This antiquated version of history was based on a biased and inaccurate viewpoint that sought to hide the origins of the human race and the secrets of the ancient past. This curriculum of lies will someday end, but until then we must continue to fight for the preservation of truth above all else.

Throughout history, countless brave individuals have been burned at the stake and silenced in order to protect this false doctrine that maintains control of our world. Some call this false doctrine of information "the system," which represents the constructs that were laid down long ago to define reality *for* us. Think about what that means for a moment. How do most people view their existence here? What is that view based on? The origins of this system can be traced back to when kingship was first lowered to Eridu in Mesopotamia, thousands of years ago. That's why learning about this forbidden knowledge is so necessary since this time period represents a rare opportunity when society has free access to this information without the fear of persecution.

In many ways, humans could be considered energetic slaves of the third dimension, incarnating repeatedly in countless bodies until we can finally grow spiritually and ascend our consciousness. The reason I use the term "slave" is that some of the beings and entities have *purposely* promoted war, distraction, and ignorance in our reality for the means of trapping mankind in an endless cycle of death and rebirth, so that they function as a type of organic battery. Sound familiar? That's one of the main reasons why those like me are fighting so hard for this information to finally be known.

Since we've covered the fundamentals of conditioning, consciousness, and the nature of reality, we must now go deeper into the ancient past to uncover the evidence that explains the true origins of the human race, as well as the real identity of these "gods" of antiquity. The first piece of evidence I want to present comes from Genesis 6:1 of the Old Testament of the Holy Bible which states:

"When people began to multiply on the face of the ground and daughters were born to them, the *sons* of God saw that they were fair; and they took wives for themselves of all that they chose. The *Nephilim* were on the earth in those days—and also afterward—when the sons of God went in to the daughters of humans, who bore children to them. These were the heroes that were of old, warriors of renown."

It's important to understand that many of the biblical

and historical perspectives that have been taught to society are derived from much older texts, such as the Atrahasis or Book of Enoch. Eventually, their original meanings became greatly diluted and altered, creating great confusion in the general population. Despite this, there is still valuable information that can be obtained within the modern Bible by studying and objectively comparing it to many of these earlier Gnostic and Mesopotamian writings in their purest forms.

A good example to show this principle can be found by reading the quote from Genesis 6:1 above, and then deciphering the terms and symbolism used within it. To break down this quote and better understand what each of these references means, we must first lay down some ground rules. The first ground rule to understand is that most references to God and the Lord in the Bible have nothing to do with what most perceive as the true "God" or conscious intelligence of the universe.

Instead, these terms are referencing certain Anunnaki beings and other entities who ruled during the Zodiac Age of Pisces. Over time, their devout followers managed to cleverly alter many of these ancient esoteric teachings to personify these beings as gods or saviors within the Abrahamic religions. This led to centuries of war and religious persecution within mankind, heralding one of the darkest times in all of human history. This information can be hard to accept, as generations of conditioning and suppression have blocked much of the truth from ever becoming known.

So, who exactly were the Nephilim? The Nephilim were considered the offspring of the Anunnaki and a mortal woman on Earth. This created a type of half-breed human that was extremely intelligent, tall, and could potentially live for hundreds, if not *thousands* of years. Evidence to support this hypothesis can be found in the Sumerian King List and Eridu Genesis with the unusually long reigns held by many of the rulers of Mesopotamia. The reason for this is due to the fact that they were considered the *direct* descendants of the Anunnaki, who evidence shows were likely tall, advanced humanoids that managed to transcend beyond the limits of the physical world. That's why there's been such a focus on preserving these ancient bloodlines in so many of the secret societies and powerful elite families that still maintain control of our world today.

The Nephilim were referred to as "giants" in the Bible, who were banished to the realm of mankind for eternity because they were considered an abomination. This is because they were created from the Anunnaki (the fallen angels) mating with mortal women, which created tall humans that could live for long periods of time. Despite being considered an abomination, they were still seen as superior to the rest of the human race, since they contained large amounts of Anunnaki DNA, and therefore were often put in places of great power over society. That's why we find evidence in cultures from Peru to Mesopotamia that many of their past kings ruled for extremely long reigns, and either had enlarged craniums or were very tall.

Based on this logic, it can be fascinating to discover that in the 1920s, large elongated skulls were found in tombs in Paracas, Peru that contained unusual DNA traits that aren't shared by *any* of the indigenous people in the region. On top of that, Peru and Bolivia contain some of the oldest and most impressive megalithic ruins in the world. Just a coincidence? Perhaps this is the missing link to help explain the influences and sophistication shared by these ancient cultures that once thrived from Easter Island and the Americas, all the way to Africa, the Middle East, and Asia.

One of the most important concepts to understand about these ancient "gods" of our past is that not *all* of them supported ignorance, war, and chaos within mankind. In fact, there developed a great rift and divide among them over the specific level of knowledge and conscious awareness that humanity was allowed to have. That's why it's so essential to separate these beings into different factions or groups, and not to simply lump them all together in the same category. The best means to determine that is to identify the particular traits, symbols, and mentalities that each of them carried throughout history.

This struggle can be seen through the principal symbols of either the eagle or the serpent, which includes variations such as the phoenix and dragon. In general, the serpent represents wisdom, spirituality, and balance, while the eagle represents strength, control, and dominance over the material world. However, to make things even more complicated, there are even depictions from early Mesopotamia that portray eagle-headed gods passing knowledge to human cultures, while in other parts of the world the serpent and dragon are playing this role. Confused yet? Allow me to explain.

These important symbols represent the divide that emerged between the Anunna over free will in mankind, as well as which bloodlines would be allowed to rule here. This competition was largely based on who should rightfully decide the fate of the human race and how these beings would be remembered. That's one of the most critical concepts to understand here, and why there's still so much confusion over whether these beings played a more benevolent or malevolent role in our reality. Evidence shows that in some cases, they actually played *both* roles.

The challenge for the Anunnaki became how they would be portrayed in the future, especially considering that some of them caused insurmountable pain and misery in the past. In many cases, those who assumed the role as the "hero" were actually the villains. After all, what really matters more than one's legacy? That's the reason why we find depictions of both the eagle and serpent spreading knowledge at different time periods, even though evidence shows that the eagle has *largely* been the great deceiver here. But wait a minute, isn't the serpent supposed to be the great deceiver? This is a topic that will be extensively discussed throughout the rest of the book.

Those who sought to provide wisdom to developing human cultures were frequently portrayed in edifices and steles holding a pine cone in one hand, and handbag in the other. That's why so many civilizations around the world depicted these symbols. An excellent example of this can be seen below in Figure 3. Notice the three horns that are present on the bottom of the helmet being worn by this tall being. This represented the status that each of them held within the Anunnaki royal hierarchy structure. The depiction below also provides clues as to what exactly the Anunna looked like in physical form, commonly shown with wings to symbolize their status as enlightened beings who mastered all of reality.

Figure 3

In Figure 3 above, notice the wrist watches, pinecone, and handbag that are shown in this Mesopotamian relief. I believe this was a symbolic representation of the role that they played in our reality as the "keepers of time and knowledge." After all, the entire concept of following a twelve-hour clock came from their direct influences. It's important to understand that what was being depicted in this relief has a symbolic meaning and purpose that often goes far beyond a linear mindset. Similar depictions can be found in cultures across the world from Mexico, Peru, and Turkey, all the way to Egypt, Iraq, and India.

The origins of these symbols can be traced back to the Fertile Crescent of Mesopotamia, where their true meanings can be understood by studying the various cylinder seals, cuneiform tablets, and edifices left behind by these ancient civilizations. To set the record straight- the eagle has *always* represented military strength, hierarchical control, and domination over the material world; while the serpent and dragon have *always* represented higher states of energy, knowledge, and the spiritual nature of reality. That's why nearly every civilization through history who portrayed an eagle or phoenix on its flag or crest, eventually became morally corrupted and driven by war and empire-building.

In the Timaeus and Critias, Plato states this is one of the major catalysts that contributed to the eventual downfall of Atlantis. This common theme is quite apparent when looking at the flags and crests of both the Spanish and Roman Empires, as well as the Nazis, Russians, and even the United States. That's why the economies of these countries often became associated with war and the conquering of other nations. This is not simply based on our natural progression over time, but evidence for the various influences these societies had in the past.

Many of the mainstream archeological "experts" teach society that these gods of the eagle and serpent are simply symbolic and shouldn't be taken literally; however, there is extensive evidence that strongly indicates to the contrary. When looking into the shared mythology of ancient cultures around the world and the knowledge that was "handed down" to them from above, it becomes clear that these symbols have meanings that go far beyond just describing the various human archetypes. In fact, eagle-headed or falcon-headed gods are frequently depicted in murals in Mexico, Pre-Dynastic Egypt, India, and Mesopotamia, right alongside the serpent and dragon. Once you recognize that pattern it can be quite shocking to discover that the gods of the eagle have seemingly defeated the gods of the serpent on Earth. That's the reason why there are so few flags and crests today that still honor the serpent and dragon. Even countries such as China and Japan, who historically worshiped the dragon, have little that remains of this great legacy any longer.

With all the misinformation and suppression that has plagued society for so long, it's somewhat surprising to learn that many of the world's flags and crests still preserve a somewhat accurate record of what occurred in history. That's why studying and recognizing the patterns found within them is so important to do. Stop for a moment and look at what symbols are portrayed on the flag or crest of the country your reading this from. Is there a serpent on it? What about an eagle, or one of its many variations that include the Byzantine or double-headed phoenix?

In fact, some of these flags and crests even portray the image of a knight slaying a serpent-dragon, which is overshadowed by the mighty double-headed phoenix. This iconic image on the Russian Coat of Arms is still present today and provides evidence to show the various influences they once had. However, I'd like to point out that these flags and crests often represent a historical record of the *past* and are not always representative of the current situation there with changing leadership. Remember, actions speak louder than words.

So, you may be wondering, what exactly happened to the higher wisdom and conscious teachings of the serpent and dragon? To some, this concept of the serpent being the "good guy" and spreading knowledge may seem backwards, but by the end of this book, I hope to prove to you without a doubt that these symbols eventually became inverted to represent their *opposite* meanings. One of the best modern examples of this can be seen with how society views the swastika. This important symbol represented eternal life, balance, and knowledge, but eventually became demonized by the Nazis and certain religions. Notice how the symbol of the serpent is still being used today by the medical industry, known as the caduceus, which represents two interwoven serpents with wings at the top. If the serpent is indeed an "evil" symbol like we've been taught, then why is it being used by one of the most prestigious institutions of all? Questions like these are an essential part of discovering the forbidden secrets of history.

The caduceus was considered by many ancient cultures to be one of the most important symbols of all, representing the ascension of human energy through the means of maintaining good health to increase one's vibration. This is achieved through a combination of acquiring higher knowledge, balancing the body's health, and reconnecting with spirituality. This information was passed down and protected by certain secret societies and groups around the world until, over time, much of it became misrepresented due to war and religious persecution. This means that in many cases, it's necessary to simply start over and relearn concepts again to gain a fresh perspective. This is not a criticism or personal attack, but an unfortunate outcome that can result from a largely deceptive and antiquated version of history that's been taught for generations.

One of the best pieces of evidence to show this can be seen with the official seal and Flag of Mexico, shown below in Figure 4.

Figure 4

The true origin and meaning behind the symbols shown on the Flag of Mexico have become nearly lost to society due to generations of deception and propaganda created after the Spanish conquered the region. Just as people in the United States are taught a greatly biased and inaccurate viewpoint regarding Christopher Columbus and the colonization of America, so too are most Mexicans regarding their true history. According to the Catholic Church, the Flag of Mexico represents the story of how the Aztec people were first led to Tenochtitlan (located on an island in the middle of Lake Texcoco) by a mighty eagle that could be seen perched on a cactus eating a snake. The Aztec were told that when they saw this eagle and serpent, that location would become their new capital city. Hmm, now doesn't that seem more than just coincidental that these particular two symbols were chosen for their flag and origin story? So, what really is the truth?

Evidence shows that the Flag of Mexico *actually* represents the historical account of how the Maya and Aztec civilizations eventually became corrupted and destroyed. First, due to the influences of these ancient "gods" of the eagle, and later by the Spanish conquistadors. This was done for the means of conquering the great serpent-dragon wisdom imparted by Kukulkan and Quetzalcoatl, as well as to gain valuable resources and lands for the Spanish Empire. Even more compelling is the fact that during this time period, one of the principal symbols shown on the Spanish flag was an eagle. These are further clues to show the influences that occurred there long ago. In the next chapter, I will be reviewing the evidence that exists to explain how the Toltec, Aztec, and Maya cultures were *all* corrupted by the same malevolent beings, known as God L and Huitzilopochtli, who tricked them into becoming war-like and practicing ritual blood sacrifice.

Looking back over the course of human history, following the rise and fall of civilizations, it's seems there has existed a hidden power struggle over control of this realm since the very beginning. This struggle reflects the conflict that emerged between what was known as "heaven" and Earth. These "overlords" of our reality, known as the Anunnaki by the Sumerians, likely structured the different astrological ages to rotate from a negative polarity low vibration to a positive polarity high vibration, as a solution to this problem. These specific energies associated with each time period were *supposed* to be rotated to preserve balance here; however, as you're about to read, that wasn't always the case.

The reason why war and evil have dominated so much of our past is due to the conflict of interest that emerged between the Anunnaki over how the time of Aries and Pisces should be governed. For those who study astrology, they may notice that the Age of Pisces is shown through the symbol of a fish and should have followed a positive polarity. This is especially true since the previous time of Aries was also negative. So, what exactly happened?

According to ancient records, some of the Anunna managed to find a way to cheat these laws of balance by allowing a negative polarity to rule the realm of Earth for two entire Zodiacal Ages. Since each astrological age lasts for 2,160 years, that means that for more than 4,000 years mankind has been *deliberately* kept in the darkness. We're just now beginning to emerge out of that chaos as we finally head towards the light of Aquarius. That's why I must point out that even though corruption and evil still largely rules our world today, great change is just over the horizon. Remember, it's always darkest just before the dawn.

This eternal dance of energy that's found within each of us is shown strikingly well in the Chinese symbol known as the yin yang. The yin yang symbol explains how seemingly opposite and dualistic forces of energy, commonly referred to as the divine masculine and feminine, are actually complementary to one another and necessary towards achieving balance. That's why evil is *always* balanced out by good in the end, since everything in the universe follows a perfect rhythm and design to it.

Due to generations of tyrannical rulers, frequent wars, and years of misinformation and propaganda, most of humanity exists in a greatly polluted version of reality that's driven by fear, hate, greed, and materialism. However, those who are more connected to their higher consciousness, empathy, and the natural world around them, will often discover this disparity and unbalance much sooner than others. Unfortunately, many of these gifted individuals often turn to a life of substance abuse or isolation to deal with the difficulty of living with this realization. The easiest way to avoid this trap is to surround yourself with like-minded individuals who will help to raise your vibration rather than lowering it. This often entails forging new relationships with people or even shedding those who are toxic. In the end, we're all here to help encourage each other to grow through the acquisition of knowledge and by realizing our *own* unique potential.

Cuneiform Tablets and Atlantean Wisdom

In order to grow on a conscious and spiritual level, it's necessary to study and understand a multitude of different esoteric teachings left behind by the temple priests and mystics from antiquity, which gives a rare glimpse into the wisdom shared by these enlightened thinkers of the past. Of all these sacred texts, the Nag Hammadi Scriptures are among the most important of all, despite the fact that few have ever heard of them. What makes the Nag Hammadi Scriptures so important, is that they represent one of the most complete Gnostic libraries ever found. Unfortunately, due to the control of information that exists, the Nag Hammadi Scriptures have been heavily suppressed ever since their discovery more than 70 years ago. I intend to rectify that by providing a brief history and summary of its contents.

In 1945, a remarkable discovery was made near the village of Hamrah Dom, Egypt when a large cache of rare Gnostic texts was discovered by two brothers in a cave near the Nile River. These Gnostic texts were known as The Nag Hammadi Scriptures, which represented ancient Egyptian wisdom that had been handed down long ago. These esoteric texts were often targeted for destruction by certain religious groups and powerful armies who wanted their contents to remain hidden. But why would so many go to these extreme lengths just to suppress this information? The reason is that the Nag Hammadi Scriptures contains forbidden knowledge that often went against the beliefs of most Abrahamic religions, explaining the true nature of reality, spirituality, and the secrets of consciousness.

The first anomaly of interest to point out about these Gnostic texts is that they were found buried in a cave that was *deliberately* sealed off from the outside world. This repetitive theme can be seen with many of the other sacred texts and esoteric teachings that have been found throughout history, such as The Book of Enoch and Dead Sea Scrolls, which strongly suggests that they needed to be protected from impending destruction. Even at the megalithic site of Gobekli Tepe in Turkey, located hundreds of miles away, we find a similar example of where a society deliberately buried something important to protect it. But from what? The answer to that question is a critical part of understanding how we got to the place we're in today.

According to evidence, there are two main reasons why these cultures would have deliberately buried these texts and sacred structures. The first is that during this time period, violent changes were occurring on the Earth which put them at great risk. The second is that they would potentially be sought for destruction by invading armies and certain religious groups in the future. It turns out that the second reason was even more dangerous than the first, as the Holy Roman Empire was deliberately seeking out these ancient texts and burning them. The underlying goal of this targeted cleanse of information was to rid the world of these Pre-Christian texts for the means of promoting a *certain* version to be supreme over the other.

That's why it's so fascinating to learn that the word "Nag" comes from the root word of "Naga" which in Sanskrit means snake. The origins of these "snake" writings can be traced back to early Egyptian societies who followed what was known as the Old Religion. The Old Religion represented the ancient spiritual teachings and wisdom that had been passed down from the time of Atlantis, more than 12,000 years ago. This knowledge was carefully guarded by the Gnostics and Druids, who were eventually hunted down and eradicated by the Holy Roman Empire and Christian church. One of the best modern examples to show this can be seen with the popular holiday known as St. Patrick's Day, where the Druid people of Ireland were brutally persecuted by the Christian church to rid their influence on the region. This led to many of these important teachings and symbols becoming inverted or demonized years later.

Contained within the second codex of the Nag Hammadi Scriptures, "The Hypothesis of the Archons" is perhaps the most intriguing chapter of all. It states that our reality is ruled by supreme beings who keep mankind enchained in their lowest state of consciousness by preying on their basic urges through the use of fear, division, and creating chaos on the planet. It's very interesting to learn that the word "archon" comes from the root word of "ruler," and that the full translation of this name is the "rulers of reality." The Hypothesis of the Archons explains that long ago, an advanced group of beings came here and took control of the realm of Earth, disrupting the natural balance that once existed. I briefly discussed this earlier in the chapter. So, the most important question is, who exactly were these *rulers of reality*?

There have been numerous references made throughout history to describe these beings by different cultures and religions across the world. The most compelling evidence can be found in ancient Mesopotamia, with the sky "gods" the Sumerians called the Anunnaki. According to the Sumerians, the Anunnaki are part of an ancient race of beings who learned to conquer the laws of reality, allowing them to transcend beyond a mortal life and exist on an interdimensional level. The "Anunna," as they call themselves in the Atrahasis, became greatly divided over disagreements they had over the future of mankind and the specific level of consciousness they should be allowed to obtain. To better understand the truth about what happened in the past, we must go back to the very beginning, to one of the oldest texts ever written known as the Emerald Tablets.

The Emerald Tablets of Thoth represent ancient Atlantean wisdom that was brought to Egypt before the time of the Dynastic pharaohs. These writings were recorded by an enlightened temple priest named Thoth, who lived in Atlantis and fled to Egypt to protect its legacy of knowledge. These teachings have been guarded by certain priests and secret societies for thousands of years who, to this day, *still* watch over the location where it's kept. That's why those who ask me where these writings can be found are often surprised by the answer I give them. This may seem strange to some, but there are those who wish to suppress or even destroy these sacred texts due to how important they are, and what they can awaken within each of us.

The Emerald Tablets of Thoth are said to have been created through a special alchemical process, which reportedly made them indestructible. As impossible as that may sound at first, it's important to understand that Thoth was considered by many to be the *greatest* alchemist of all time. Thoth was the creator of the early civilizations of Khemet, also called Khem, which later became known as Egypt. The name "Khem" is likely derived from the root word of "alchemy", which shows how significant the practice of alchemy was to these Pre-Dynastic cultures of Egypt.

According to ancient stories, Thoth originally placed the Emerald Tablets in a special chamber found inside the Great Pyramid of Giza, until it was eventually moved to a secret location within one of the temples in Teotihuacan, Mexico. Over time, those who have been tasked with guarding its location have gone to great lengths to protect its contents. Even the famous physicist Isaac Newton extensively studied the Hermetic version of these tablets, which may have influenced some of his later theories. To those who don't think they're genuine, I advise that you simply read the words for yourself in order to truly understand their importance.

Tablet 1 of the Emerald Tablets states:

"I, Thoth, the Atlantean, master of mysteries,
keeper of records, mighty king, magician,
living from generation to generation,
being about to pass into the halls of Amenti,
set down for the guidance of
those that are to come after,
these records of the mighty wisdom of Great Atlantis.

In the great city of Keor on the island of Undal,
in a time far past, I began this incarnation.
Not as the little men of the present age did
the mighty ones of Atlantis live and die,
but rather from aeon to aeon did they renew
their life in the Halls of Amenti where the river of life
flows eternally onward.

A hundred times ten
have I descended the dark way that led into light,
and as many times have I ascended from the
darkness into the light my strength and power renewed.

Now for a time I descend,
and the men of Khem
shall know me no more.

But in a time yet unborn will I rise again,
mighty and potent, requiring an accounting
of those left behind me."

Tablet 2 of the Emerald Tablets states:

"Far in a past time, lost in the space time,
the Children of Light looked down on the world.
Seeing the children of men in their bondage,
bound by the force that came from beyond.
Knew they that only by freedom from bondage
could man ever rise from the Earth to the Sun.

Down they descended and created bodies,
taking the semblance of men as their own.
The Masters of everything said after their forming:

"We are they who were formed from the space-dust,
partaking of life from the infinite All;
living in the world as children of men,
like and yet unlike the children of men."

Then for a dwelling place, far 'neath the earth crust,
blasted great spaces they by their power,
spaces apart from the children of men.
Surrounded them by forces and power,
shielded from harm they the Halls of the Dead.

Side by side then, placed they other spaces,
filled them with Life and with Light from above.
Builded they then the Halls of Amenti,
that they might dwell eternally there,
living with life to eternity's end.

Thirty and two were there of the children,
sons of Lights who had come among men,

seeking to free from the bondage of darkness
those who were bound by the force from beyond."

The information contained within the first two Emerald Tablets helps to shed light on a nearly lost time period in human history, one that's still largely clouded in mystery. It helps to fill in many of the gaps we still have regarding soul incarnation, energy, and the identity of who these "Children of Light" are who descended into our reality long ago. Thoth goes on to explain that when these Children of Light arrived here they were divided into playing certain roles, ruling over either the upper dimensions or lower dimensions. Enki was assigned the ruler of the underworld, where he went to reside deep within what they called the "abzu." That's how he became associated with Satan by the church. One of the things I find most fascinating about the second Emerald Tablet is when it mentions the age of these "Children of Light," stating they were "formed from the space-dust."

The details provided within the Emerald Tablets is very similar to both the Atrahasis and Enuma Elish, which gives strong credibility to the factual nature of its content. I find it unfortunate and somewhat sad that many haven't done the research needed to fully appreciate the significance of these ancient texts. Instead, many choose to blindly go along with the false narrative which has been spoon fed to them for years, which unequivocally states that human civilization emerged around 6,000 years ago, and is derived from nothing more than intelligent apes. Evidence strongly indicates that this couldn't be further from the truth.

Geneticist experts, such as Lloyd Pye have pointed out that Homo sapiens contain a total of only 46 chromosomes, instead of the 48 found in most primates. This is peculiar since it appears that at some point in our history, two of our chromosomes were fused together. This fusing together of our chromosomes would be impossible in nature, which supports the theory that humans were created through the means of genetic manipulation. To better understand the events which led to the disappearance of many of the megalithic civilizations around the world, as well as the truth behind the origins of the human race, we turn to the Mesopotamian cuneiform tablets that make up the Epic of Atrahasis.

Out of the thousands of ancient texts that have been recovered in the last several hundred years, the Atrahasis may be the *most* important of them all. This is due to the sheer amount of information it provides regarding the Anunnaki and the human origin story, as well as the violent events that occurred at the end of the Younger Dryas. Before we delve into the actual tablets themselves, I want to provide some background into who Atrahasis was. The name Atrahasis means, "exceedingly wise," and was written from the perspective of a past king who ruled in Sumer, just before the events of the great flood. He was called by many names, including Ziusudra in the Sumerian King List, or Utnapishtim in the Epic of Gilgamesh. His father was known as Ubara-Tutu, who was *one* of the last kings of Sumer.

It's important that I point out that some of the older translations of the Sumerian King List state that Ubara-Tutu was the last king of Shuruppak; however newer revisions show that Ziusudra, his son, likely ruled after him for a brief amount of time before the flood occurred. Either way, the evidence clearly points to the fact that both Ziusudra and Ubara-Tutu were closely related and both alive *before* the great flood. This means that they're a vital part of what's known as our Antediluvian or Pre-Diluvian past. This is important because it represents a rare look into the events that occurred during a nearly lost time period in human history, which in many ways is still largely unknown to most of society.

Essentially, the account of the flood told through Atrahasis became the religious story of Noah and the ark. Just as with many other cuneiform tablets from Mesopotamia, the stories they contain were altered by the church until they no longer resembled their original form. In my opinion, this was done for the means of hiding certain key pieces of information found within them, that if discovered, could greatly disrupt the false doctrine we've been taught. As I've stated previously, this false narrative and timeline is tightly guarded by powerful individuals in the upper echelons of our governments, who refuse to allow the truth of our past to be revealed.

These cuneiform tablets were written by the Sumerian and Babylonian civilizations of Mesopotamia, who are known as some of the oldest civilizations on the planet. That's why the information they contain should be held with the highest regard by academics and not simply left on museum shelves and in basements to gather dust. Cuneiform is a style of writing where symbols and letters are etched into stone or clay so that their message can be preserved long into the future. Unlike paper, which has a relatively short lifespan, these cuneiform tablets can withstand fire and even devastating floods, which is the only reason why they're still around today.

The nearly unknown Ashurbanipal Library, found in the ruins of the city of Nineveh, Iraq in 1849, contained the largest gathering of Mesopotamian cuneiform texts in the world, which included both the Atrahasis and Enuma Elish. The Ashurbanipal Library was eventually burned to the ground by invading armies from Babylon, but unlike the Library of Alexandria in Egypt, which was made up of almost entirely paper records, the majority of the cuneiform tablets from Nineveh survived the fire.

So, you may be wondering, what exactly does the Atrahasis look like? Figure 5 below shows the cuneiform tablets which make up the Epic of Atrahasis.

Figure 5

Over time, many of these ancient cuneiform records were either damaged or lost, leaving only fragments and clues today that can tell us what occurred thousands of years ago. To read compelling evidence that *directly* mentions the Anunnaki, as well as explaining mankind's origins, we will review the tablets that make up the Atrahasis. The following translation of the Atrahasis was done by leading experts in their field, including George Smith and Stephanie Dalley, and should be viewed as highly accurate and credible. Carefully read and ponder these words for yourself to discover their hidden meanings.

Tablet 1 of the Atrahasis states:

"When the gods instead of man
Did the work, bore the loads,
The gods' load was too great,
The work too hard, the trouble too much.
They took and cast the lots; the gods made the division.
Anu went up to the sky, and Enlil took the earth for his people.
The bolt which bars the sea was assigned to far-sighted Enki.
When Anu had gone up to the sky,
And the gods of the Apsu had gone below,
The Anunnaki of the sky made the Igigi bear the workload.
The Igigi gods had to dig out canals,
Had to clear channels, the lifelines of the land.
For 3,600 years they bore the excess.
Hard work, night and day.
They groaned and blamed each other,
Come, let us carry Enlil,
The counselor of the gods, the warrior, from his

dwelling.
And get him to relieve us of our hard work!
Now, cry battle!
Let us mix fight with battle!
The Igigi set fire to their tools,
Put aside their spades for fire.

When they reached the gate of warrior Enlil's dwelling,
It was night, the middle watch,
Ekur was surrounded, Enlil had not realized.

Enlil sent for Anu to be brought down to him,
Enki was fetched into his presence,
Anu, king of the sky was present,
Enki, king of the Apsu attended.
All the great Anunnaki were present.

The Igigi declared,
"Every single one of us declared war!
We have put a stop to the digging.
The load is excessive, it is killing us!

Anu made his voice heard and spoke to the gods his
brothers,
"What are we complaining of?
Their work was indeed too hard, their trouble was too
much."

Ea made his voice heard and spoke;
"Let us create a mortal man
So that he may bear the yoke, the work of Enlil,
Let man bear the load of the gods."

Nintu made her voice heard, and spoke;
"On the first, seventh, and fifteenth of the month
I shall make a purification by washing.
Then one god should be slaughtered.
Then a god and a man will be mixed together in clay.
Let a ghost come into existence from the god's flesh
And let the ghost exist so as not to forget the slain god."

Tablet 1 of the Atrahasis provides some of the most detailed information we have for the true origin story of mankind, as well as the identity of who these "gods of the Apsu" really were. It explains the reason why scientists find a missing link in the evolutionary timeline of Homo sapiens, as well as how the human brain could have doubled in size over a very short time period. Notice at the end of the tablet when the term "ghost" is used to reference the development of consciousness and a soul within the body. The real question is, how could these cultures have known about this information more than 10,000 years ago if they had *no* outside influences? The logical conclusion to make, based on reading these tablets and studying history, is that these civilizations were *given* this information from a supreme race of beings. But who exactly were they? Let's review what we know about these beings who call themselves the Anunna.

According to Mesopotamian cuneiform texts and cylinder seals, the Anunnaki came to the realm of Earth to free themselves from the burden of needing a physical body, as well as to harness its abundant electromagnetic energy. However, they eventually realized that they still needed physical beings to maintain the planet after the

Igigi, known as the Watchers in the Book of Enoch, eventually revolted and demanded relief. In fact, the exhausting labor involved with building infrastructure and maintaining our world is well documented in the Atrahasis, where it explains in great detail the grueling work involved with digging out and clearing the silt from the river systems used for agriculture. Records indicate that these events may have occurred more than *100,000* years ago. So, you may be wondering, what's so special about this planet?

The Earth is what's known as a terrestrial planet, which means that it's primarily composed of quartz-rich rocks and metals that developed slowly over billions of years from intense heat and pressure. This is an important fact to consider, as these types of rocks were almost *exclusively* used within the megalithic structures that were built around the world. Due to the properties of quartz, some of these masons and builders were known to have traveled more than 100 hundred miles to acquire them, and in some rare cases over 500 miles. This meant sometimes moving stones that were in excess of 1000 tons over great distances. But how exactly could they have achieved this impossible feat? This evidence strongly indicates that these human civilizations were influenced long ago by the beings referred to in the Atrahasis as the Anunna.

Since disasters and extinctions have occurred throughout Earth's history, from the combination of tectonic changes, solar activity, and cosmic impacts, life had to frequently start over from scratch. To me, the *only* plausible explanation that makes sense for how so many lifeforms could have survived these disastrous events is if outside intervention played a role. That's why so many

Mesopotamian cuneiform tablets and Gnostic texts indicate that these beings disrupted the delicate balance that once existed here. According to the tablets of the Atrahasis, these beings refer to themselves as the "Great Anunna," who eventually created mankind to alleviate the "workload of the gods." Is it any surprise then that the human genome contains so many strange anomalies whose origins can't be explained by most experts? These anomalies in the human genome are referred to as "non-coding DNA" or "junk DNA," which means that it's not shared by *any* other species on the planet.

Besides quartz-rich rocks, the Anunna, as well as certain kings and pharaohs of antiquity, may have been interested in acquiring rare earth elements such as gold and diamonds. That doesn't mean that I support the theory that the Anunnaki needed gold to fix the atmosphere of their dying planet, as Sitchin suggests, but I have found evidence that emphasizes the importance of these elements to many of these ancient civilizations. But for what purpose? This is where understanding the properties of the periodic table and alchemy can be beneficial. If one reads the Emerald Tablets, they will quickly notice the significance that alchemy played to many of these past cultures, especially the Egyptians and Atlanteans. These elements were not only used to potentially heal and extend one's lifespan, but some of them may have been *essential* components within the advanced drills and saws used to create these precise megalithic structures. Remember, the only way to effectively cut these quartz-rich, granite stone blocks would be with a tool that's harder than the material you're working with. That's how we know that these civilizations didn't create them using bronze-age tools.

Out of the nearly one hundred natural elements found on the period table, gold and diamonds contain some of the more unique properties of all. Despite the role that these elements played within alchemy and in certain technologies used today, most are unaware of their true value and largely regard them as nothing more than attractive or rare. However, if one was to do a little research into the atomic properties of rare metals such as gold, they may be quite shocked with what they find. Gold, or Au as it's referred to on the periodic table, is considered a superconductor of electricity and is one of the only elements that's ever been discovered which is truly eternal, meaning it won't break down or degrade over time. These unique properties may be one of the main reasons why gold was so sought after throughout history, including the obsession that developed over discovering the secrets of the philosopher's stone.

Some of the pharaohs of Egypt that were discovered within the Valley of the Kings were buried alongside what's known as Monoatomic gold-or Ormus gold. Ormus gold is created through an alchemical process that converts gold into a powder form that's consumed to extend one's life. Is this how the kings mentioned in the Sumerian King List were able to rule for such extended periods of time or was it related to genetics? Regardless, these unique properties of gold mean that it may literally be the "Holy Grail" of immortality for any biological being in the universe. We may have only scratched the surface in understanding the significance that gold played to many of the kings and rulers of the past. That's why it's so interesting to learn that some experts postulate that the Earth may contain the *most* gold out of any planet in the Solar System. Curious isn't it? Instead of viewing gold as just another rare and attractive metal, we should see it as one of the most vital and important elements of all.

In order to help explain these unusual properties of gold, consider for a moment the idea of a Spanish ship that's full of gold, silver, and copper bullion, traveling back across the Atlantic Ocean after conquistadors had plundered it from the native cultures. During the voyage, the ship sinks in a violent storm, sending all the cargo to the bottom of the ocean, where it remains untouched for hundreds of years. Eventually, a dive team discovers the wreckage and recovers the cargo. As the sunken treasure is revealed in the sunlight, the crew members shockingly discover that the copper has turned green and the silver has turned black; this is due to a chemical process that occurs to these metals when they become exposed to certain amounts of iron, sulfur, and hydrogen over time. That's why today the Statue of Liberty in New York City is green and not copper-color. But what about the gold? The dive team that recovered the sunken treasure is astonished to find that the gold is as shiny and yellow as the day it was first taken out of the ground, even though it sat at the bottom of the ocean for hundreds of years.

Along with its eternal qualities, gold is also highly reflective, which means that it can reflect nearly 100% of incoming solar radiation. That means that gold would be an *essential* component needed for any biological being attempting space travel. The reason for this is because no other element found on the periodic table would be able to adequately reflect the extreme radiation and heat that occurs upon leaving the atmosphere of a planet. Today, gold is extensively used by modern astronauts within their spaceships, visors, and suits, which shows its overall importance to space travel. Gold is also highly effective as a conductor of electricity, which is why it's considered vital within countless electronic devices such as computers, televisions, and cell phones. However, the real value of gold may not simply be from its extensive technological uses, but from its secrets pertaining to human aging. Hopefully, one day, we will re-discover these eternal properties of gold, or perhaps we already have.

Mesopotamian cuneiform tablets state that the Anunna were governed by a male-dominated kingship hierarchy, which was directly based on specific royal bloodlines and family heritage. Sound familiar? That's why "kingship" is so frequently mentioned in these ancient texts, such as the Sumerian King List and Legend of Etana, since this was the model that was *chosen* for developing human civilizations to follow. After thousands of years of royal kings and queens ruling in a hierarchy pyramid structure, it's clear that it's still largely in place even today. Try not to be fooled by the illusion of democracy and open government, and instead see the bigger picture for who is *really* in charge.

The purpose of this particular style of governing was to both mimic their kingship structure, as well as to protect certain bloodline descendants that could continuously rule and maintain their best interests. Wait a second, isn't that precisely what's happened with the conquistadors and empires of history? Traditionally, after an army conquers another nation, they enact their own laws and governing structure that mirrors their own. In almost every case, this structure is based on a hierarchy kingship model. The conquering of the Aztec, Maya, and Inca cultures is a great example to prove this point. Now you may be wondering, how do the Igigi fit into all of this?

According to cuneiform records, the Igigi were the non-royal demigods of the Anunnaki, who acted as a type of servant or emissary for them. The Atrahasis states that the Igigi labored on Earth for thousands of years, clearing river channels and building structures, until eventually they revolted and demanded relief from the hard work. That's why the decision was made to create humans in the first place, to fulfill the role of the Igigi here. In the Book of Enoch, the Igigi were known as "The Watchers," who constantly observe the events on Earth and the progress of mankind. Some of these beings have the ability to exist in higher dimensions, just like the Anunna, which is why they became associated with angels or archangels by many religions. The reason the Igigi are tasked with monitoring the human race is due to the disparity that exists with the Anunna over *our* perception of time. I will be discussing this area in further detail throughout the course of the book.

The Book of Enoch goes into great detail discussing these "fallen angels," who came down to the realm of Earth to breed with the daughters of men. The result of this promiscuous act led to the creation of the Nephilim, who were known as the giants in the Book of Genesis. Evidence to support this hypothesis can be found in the King James version of the Bible, which states:

"There were giants in the earth in those days; and also after that, when the sons of God came in unto the daughters of men, and they bare children to them, the same became mighty men which were of old, men of renown."

As I discussed previously, the Nephilim were known as the giants of ancient history, who were created through the process of these beings mating with human women on Earth. That's why so many cuneiform records state that certain kings were "chosen" to rule since they were considered the direct descendants of the Anunnaki. This is where the obsession over specific bloodlines first began, and the reason so many of the past kings from Mesopotamia were portrayed as being extremely tall and ruling for *thousands* of years in the Sumerian King List. A great example of this can be seen with the story of Atrahasis (Ziusudra), who was saved from the deluge because he was considered a descendant of Enki.

In fact, going even a step further, the famous hero known as Gilgamesh, who was a king of Uruk, was often depicted in murals holding a full-grown pet lion that looks no bigger than a house cat. The way we can tell that the lion is full grown is because it has a mane. Only mature male lions can have a mane. This provides a basis for just how tall these past rulers were, and why Sumerian cylinder seals portray the Anunnaki as being so much taller than the human servants and priests around them. These hybrid humans, known as the Nephilim or giants, were banished to live amongst mankind because their inception was considered a sin. That's how the Anunnaki became associated with *fallen angels* by many religions of history. While I understand that the idea of giant humans may be difficult for some to accept, allow me to share some additional evidence that supports these conclusions.

When the famous explorer Magellan was sailing through the southern region of Patagonia in 1520, his party reported that they encountered giant men, some over ten feet tall, who fiercely attacked them when they came ashore. Magellan's men were forced to leave the area and continue on their journey, but when they returned home they reported the incident. This information came from the actual log entries of the world-famous sailor Magellan himself, yet it was *somehow* left out of our textbooks. However, the objective researcher can still find details from this encounter when researching the area named after him, known as: "The Strait of Magellan."

Besides Magellan, there have been numerous records made that directly mention giants, such as the Romans, who supposedly encountered and fought them in bloody battles while traveling through the forests of Germania. Despite this, nearly all information regarding this subject was eventually covered up and hidden due to the sensitive nature of what it represented. Today, most people just gawk or laugh at the idea of giant humans living in the past. That's one of the main reasons why the teachings found within the Book of Enoch were kept secret and deliberately left out of the modern bible. Someday in the future, when these records are finally released from secure locations such as the Vatican Archives, giants will no longer be considered just a myth and will be an important part of our history. You may be wondering now how this relates to the origin story of mankind. Let's continue with the Atrahasis to find answers.

The Origins of Mankind

The cuneiform tablets of the Atrahasis explain that after the revolt of the Igigi, the twelve royal Anunna council members were summoned to discuss what needed to be done to satisfy the manual labor on the planet. After extensive thought, a solution was decided upon to create a primitive worker to handle the necessary labor, instead of the Igigi. The wise Ea, also known as Enki, lobbied the council to use the primitive Denisovan and Neanderthal beings to fulfill this role. The Denisovan and Neanderthal early hominids then became the model used for creating the modern-day Homo sapien. The Anunnaki council of twelve later decided to alter the genome of these native pre-hominid species to jumpstart its evolution using their own DNA.

Records and evidence indicate that this tampering in the genome of early hominids occurred more than 200,000 years ago, through utilizing their vast understanding of both technology and DNA sequencing. After extensive trial and error, several root races of humans were created which were dispersed throughout different regions of the planet. According to Mesopotamian cuneiform tablets, Enlil instructed Ea to create a primitive worker that was *only* intelligent enough to comprehend and take basic orders. Enlil was concerned that if mankind were to become too smart, they would begin to ask too many questions and could eventually realize the truth about their past and who they really are.

Unbeknownst to Enlil, his half-brother Ea, along with help from Mami, decided to secretly design a model of Homo sapien that was extremely intelligent and contained large amounts of Anunnaki DNA. That's where the term "mommy," or "mother" originates from as she was considered the mother of mankind. The goddess Mami was known as Ninmah or Ninhursag to the Mesopotamians, and Isis to the Egyptians. Together, both Ea and Mami felt great responsibility and compassion for their creation and enacted certain fail-safe methods to ensure that the human race wouldn't become enslaved by false ideas and their primitive urges in the future.

The way this was achieved was by designing special chakra centers of energy within the human body, found along the spinal cord, that could become activated to raise consciousness levels based on natural cycles that occur in the Solar System. That meant that the human species had the potential to rival or even become greater than their creators. This led to tension and anger within some of the Anunna, who proceeded to create chaos and war on the planet to prevent this ascension of human energy from ever taking place. Evidence shows that due to this perceived risk, some of these malevolent beings may have even gone back in to further tamper with the human genome, to attempt to unplug these chakra centers and lower human intelligence. However, despite their best efforts, it's clear that mankind is becoming more aware and conscious every day.

To truly verify that the information in the Atrahasis is accurate, we need more sources of evidence that support it. We find that evidence in another set of Mesopotamian cuneiform tablets known as Enuma Elish, which were found alongside the Atrahasis in the Ashurbanipal Library. This not only helps to provide additional evidence to prove the origins of the human race but also gives credibility to both of these ancient texts. So now you may be wondering, what exactly does the Enuma Elish say?

Reading from **Tablet 6** of the Enuma Elish it states:

"They bound him, holding him before Ea.
They inflicted the penalty on him and severed his blood-vessels.
From his blood he, Ea created mankind,
On whom he imposed the service of the gods, and set the gods free
After the wise Ea had created mankind
And had imposed the service of the gods upon them—
That task is beyond comprehension
The gods were then divided,
All the Anunnaki into upper and lower groups.
He assigned 300 in the heavens to guard the decrees of Anu and appointed them as a guard."

Tablet 6 of the Enuma Elish provides further evidence to show that the human genome was altered long ago by great beings who call themselves the Anunna. This information helps to answer important questions regarding the purpose of the non-coding DNA found in humans, as well as the reason for our abnormally large brain size. Someday in the future, when the veil is lifted regarding the secrets of the past and mankind's true origins, the collective of humanity will finally be able to separate itself from the animal kingdom and realize their inherent responsibility as stewards of the Earth. This is the underlying reason why Thoth refers to humans as the children of men since most refuse to grow up and accept the truth of who they really are.

When Enlil found out that Ea and Mami had secretly designed the human genome to contain their unique gifts and the ability to obtain higher states of consciousness, he was furious and promised to never allow them to reach their full potential. This decision made by Ea and Mami to take the side of both pity and compassion towards the human race would create a great divide among the Anunna, which acted as the main catalyst behind the struggle we see throughout history that I call: "the eagle versus the serpent."

In Mesopotamian cuneiform tablets, Enlil frequently refers to mankind as "beasts" who are unworthy of the divine gifts they had been given. When Enlil was chosen to become the ruler of the physical realm of Earth, instead of his half-brother Ea, a plot to enslave humanity by preying on their primitive urges and trapping them in the material world was orchestrated and carried out. This was done through the means of conditioning society to exist in a paradigm based on war, fear, and a false understanding of the true nature of reality. Although he is often portrayed as a major player in these malevolent activities towards mankind, it's important to point out that Enlil wasn't the only being involved in this deceptive plot against human awareness; as there have been other beings and entities who have also played a role. As difficult as that may be to accept, we must understand that not all beings and entities in the universe have humanity's best intentions in mind.

The story of The Garden of Eden speaks to this inner conflict that exists between the Anunna over the future of consciousness in mankind, which is represented through the symbolism of the serpent and God figure. This famous story is also one of the oldest references ever made connecting Ea (Enki) to the symbol of the snake, and Enlil to the figure of God. The decision given to Adam and Eve from the serpent about whether or not to eat from the tree of knowledge led to them being banned from the garden for eternity to wander *alone* in a state of ignorance and confusion.

This banning from the "garden" symbolically represented the human race forging its own path through free will, without the aid of these deities and higher beings. The clever trick used by organized religion regarding the interpretation of this story was to make society believe that the serpent is evil and that the God figure is divine and assisting humanity. This inversion of the facts couldn't be further from the truth and would lead humanity down a path of darkness that would span thousands of years. We're just now finally emerging from this great deception that has plagued us for so long.

Going deeper into the story of Adam and Eve, God (or in this case Enlil) doesn't want humans to know of good or evil, but to instead live in a primitive state of awareness, governed by ignorance and misinformation. Adam and Eve ultimately decide they want higher consciousness and free will, thanks to the sacrifices made by the serpent, known as Ea. Enlil banishes Homo sapiens to a life of bondage and slavery through the creation of certain laws and rules, which act to divide mankind by separating the languages and races on the planet in order to trap them in an endless cycle of inner conflict.

To avoid society discovering the truth and uprising, people were kept in a perpetual state of total ignorance and confusion about the past, where constant distractions prevented them from reaching higher states of awareness. However, these methods were largely unsuccessful and Enlil and others quickly realized that they needed to take further action to slow down the progression of their conscious evolution. The solution they came up with was to tamper with the human genome, by infusing DNA from a species similar to what's today called the rhesus monkey. This led to a "dumbing down" of the human genome, causing it to function in a reduced state of awareness by unplugging the important chakra centers found in the body.

This tampering of the human genome divided mankind into two major blood group systems known as either Rh+ or Rh-. What that means is that if your blood is tested as Rh-, then you don't have the Rh antigens present. It's important to point out that the Rh factor differs from the primary ABO blood group system and is *not* normally tested outside of pregnant women. Today, around 85% of the world's population is Rh+, which may help to explain why we see such a large discrepancy in the levels of awareness. However, these individuals who are Rh+ still have the same potential as anyone else for reaching higher states of consciousness. The only difference is they may have a harder time achieving those goals. When the human genome was altered and tampered with, the result was that the double-helix DNA and chakra centers became split apart and unplugged, which greatly limited the potential for our energetic and spiritual growth.

Despite all these disruptions, the collective consciousness of humanity is starting to change on a fundamental level, becoming more aware every day thanks in part to the internet and the freedom of information. The difficult questions that were once ignored and cared little about by most are now relevant and important. This forbidden knowledge that has been held back for centuries is being met with a combination of anger, shock, and curiosity. After years of deception, misinformation, and false conditioning, the true nature of our existence here is finally becoming realized. The notion of organized conspiracies and deception may be uncomfortable for some to consider, but like all great stories, ours is just beginning.

Thoth and other enlightened thinkers of the past have commonly referred to the human race as "the children of mankind" because they considered us like children who are constantly struggling to conquer the illusions of the material world and discover who we really are. Carl Jung once famously said, "People will do anything, no matter how absurd, to avoid facing their own souls." This quote speaks volumes to explain why there is such a lack of motivation in society for self-improvement and reaching greater states of awareness. The underlying message to take away from this is that the road leading to higher states of consciousness and spiritual ascension is extremely challenging and because of that, many will not succeed. That unfortunate outcome means that only a small percentage of people will fully understand the significance of this information, while most will instead reject or choose to ignore it.

In the next chapter, we will travel around the world to the review the evidence that shows the struggle of the

eagle and serpent throughout history, the details of the cataclysms that occurred during the Younger Dryas, and the war in heaven by the Anunna.
(1,2,3,8,9,10,11,13,14,15,16,17,18,19,20)

CHAPTER 3

ANUNNA, EAGLE AND SERPENT, AND DELUGE

I would like to start this chapter by citing an important quote from Manly P. Hall, which helps to exemplify the importance of symbolism to history. "When the human race learns to read the language of symbolism, a great veil will fall from the eyes of men. They shall then know truth and, more than that, they shall realize that from the beginning truth has been in the world unrecognized, save by a small but gradually increasing number appointed by the Lords of the Dawn as ministers to the needs of human creatures struggling to regain their consciousness of divinity."

After years of extensively studying the specific symbolism found within ancient murals, cylinder seals, and flags and crests around the planet, it became clear to me that the eagle and serpent represent far more than what we've been told. On the highest level, this struggle represents the eternal conflict that exists within mankind over whether it will continue to be blinded by the illusions of the physical world through the means of war, distraction, and material gain, or discover the secrets of consciousness and embrace the essence of their spiritual nature. This "war" is being fought over in both the higher and lower dimensions by the Anunnaki, as well as *other* beings, which is then manifested down into the third dimension of our reality. Hence the term, "as above so below." You may be asking yourself, what is the evidence that shows this is real and not simply just a representation of the various human archetypes? Over the course of this chapter, I will be presenting you with extensive evidence that supports these theories.

Before we go any further, the first point that must be understood about this struggle is that it only exists due to the universal law of *free will*. Mortal man is governed by certain laws and rules such as free will, which allows each of us to choose whatever decisions we want, both mentally and physically. These decisions determine our ultimate path in life. This conflict of interest within mankind led the Anunna to become split apart into two distinct factions, represented by either the eagle or serpent. In many ways, these symbols can also be equated to the properties of darkness and light, good or evil, and knowledge versus ignorance. Due to the properties of free will, changes to consciousness, and the unpredictability of human emotions, each person has the potential to change their mind at any time, and often without a logical reason. This became one of the great challenges for some of the Anunnaki, as they attempted to manage how we perceive reality.

After reviewing the specific symbolism and mentality that has dominated human societies for the last 2,000 years, the unfortunate conclusion one would logically have to come to is that the influences of the serpent have seemingly lost this struggle here. But the real question is, for how long? In order to better understand this eternal struggle found within the Anunna, as well as what lies ahead for our future, we need to travel back through the events of history by objectively following the breadcrumb trail of evidence.

According to Mesopotamian cuneiform tablets, hundreds of thousands of years ago a great rivalry emerged between the Anunnaki half-brothers of Ea and Enlil, along with the various offspring each of them had. Their differing mentalities towards mankind created tense competition and chaos on the planet due to this ongoing war in the "heavens." Eventually, a decision was made by their elder leader Anu to separate this family feud by designating each of them to rule over certain territories and domains on Earth. That's the reason why these symbols can be found in so many different cultures across the world.

Because Enki was known as the spiritual healer, magician, intellectual, and balancer of energy for the Anunna, he was designated as the ruler of the abzu, which included the fresh water, oceans, and underworld. Ea (or Enki as he was later known), was designated as the ruler of the non-physical world, which meant balancing the energy cycles of the Earth, along with the conscious and spiritual levels in mankind. His symbols became the serpent and dragon, which represented knowledge, wisdom, and eternal balance. This legacy of wisdom left behind by Enki and Thoth can still be seen today through the medical caduceus symbol, which can be found on most ambulances and hospitals. Despite the demonization and inversion that occurred to the serpent over time, we must always remember how it was originally represented by ancient civilizations and mystery schools of antiquity.

In fact, the word "nagas" was often used in India and southeast Asia to describe the various adept masters, or Rishi, who sought to acquire higher knowledge for achieving greater states of awareness. The term "nagas" fully translates to mean "serpent worshipers," which can be traced back to the origins of early Gnosticism, Hinduism, and Buddhism. These Rishi were also referred to as seers, sages, or mystics, who closely followed the serpent teachings that had been passed down from long ago from the civilizations of Atlantis and Pre-Dynastic Egypt.

The Druids of Ireland, Scotland, and England also believed that the symbol of the serpent represented the ultimate balance of knowledge, energy, and spirituality. That's the reason why they were eventually eradicated from the region by Saint Patrick, who referred to them as the "snakes." When you consider the fact that "pure" light represents the combination of all seven colors of the visible light spectrum, it helps to connect and explain why we find statues across India and Asia that portray a snake with seven heads. Not to mention that one of the most famous secret societies in all of history was known as the Brotherhood of the Snake.

Going deeper, the philosopher Plato describes Atlantis as being a landmass that contained seven principal islands. Considering that all these sacred cultures worshipped the teachings of the serpent and light, it's clear that this was no accident. The Egyptians even claim that they were the direct descendants of the people of

Atlantis, who according to Thoth, traveled to the land of Khem to rebuild their society and protect this important knowledge after cataclysms destroyed their home. The reason Plato knew so much about Atlantis was from studying these ancient records. Just like the Atlanteans, the Egyptians also worshipped the symbol of the serpent, which was commonly shown coiled above the crowns of great pharaohs and depicted in many of their murals.

Further east in Asia, the serpent was extensively worshipped, but in a slightly different way than in Egypt and India. Instead of the symbol of the snake, it was depicted as a dragon, which represented the metamorphosis of the serpent into its highest form. This common theme of "transformation" is best seen in the Maya, Aztec, and Inca cultures of the Americas, where the wisdom bringers from Atlantis influenced the god(s) of Kukulkan, Quetzalcoatl, and Viracocha. All of these names translate to mean: "plumed" or "feathered" serpents, and in many ways, all reference the same thing. That's why throughout history, nearly every civilization that based itself on acquiring wisdom and higher knowledge was represented by the serpent and dragon. Sadly, over time, these sacred symbols were eventually demonized by the church and inverted to their opposite meaning.

Along with the cultures of the Americas, this common theme showing the transformation of human consciousness was also echoed thousands of miles away by the Egyptians, who portrayed this important knowledge in murals as coiled serpents with wings. That's the reason why the medical caduceus symbol still shows the coiled serpent with wings at the top, to represent achieving optimal health in the body. This is a necessary component when seeking to maintain higher states of consciousness and energy. Quickly, you begin to recognize that all this knowledge is interconnected across countless cultures on the planet, spanning entire continents and oceans, who all share these common influences from the past. As Manly P. Hall eloquently stated, much of this knowledge has been cleverly hidden within complex metaphors and symbols, that patiently wait for a time when the collective of humanity can once again rediscover these secrets of consciousness and ascension.

Manly P. Hall was a brilliant writer and thinker who carried on the great legacy of Hermes, by passing along this ancient Egyptian wisdom into the future. To further understand these influences and connections back to the symbol of the serpent and dragon, we must study the hermetic writings known as: "The Life and Teachings of Thoth Hermes Trismegistus." In these important writings, the famous Hermetic tail of *Poimandres* helps to clarify both who the great dragon Poimandres is, along with the identity of the Egyptian god Osiris. The following is a reading from *Poimandres, The Vision of Hermes:*

"Following the secret instructions of the Temple, Hermes gradually freed his higher consciousness from the bondage of his bodily senses; and, thus released, his divine nature revealed to him the mysteries of the transcendental spheres. He beheld a figure, terrible and awe-inspiring. It was the Great Dragon, with wings stretching across the sky and light streaming in all directions from its body. The Great Dragon called Hermes by name and asked him why he thus meditated upon the World Mystery. Terrified by the spectacle, Hermes prostrated himself before the Dragon, beseeching it to reveal its identity. The great creature answered that it was Poimandres, the Mind of the Universe, the Creative Intelligence, and the Absolute Emperor of all. Hermes then besought Poimandres to disclose the nature of the universe and the constitution of the gods.

Understand, O Hermes, and meditate deeply upon the mystery. That which in you sees and hears is not of the earth, but is the Word of God incarnate. So it is said that Divine Light dwells in the midst of mortal darkness, and ignorance cannot divide them. The union of the Word and the Mind produces that mystery which is called *Life*. As the darkness without you is divided against itself, so the darkness within you is likewise divided. The Light and the fire which rise are the divine man, ascending in the path of the Word, and that which fails to ascend is the mortal man, which may not partake of immortality. Learn deeply of the Mind and its mystery, for therein lies the secret of immortality.

Hermes asked if all men did not have Minds, and the Great Dragon replied: 'Take heed what you say, for I am the Mind--the Eternal Teacher. I am the Father of the *Word*--the Redeemer of all men--and in the nature of the wise the Word takes flesh. By means of the Word, the world is saved. I, *Thought*--the Father of the Word, the Mind--come only unto men that are holy and good, pure and merciful, and that live piously and religiously, and my presence is an inspiration and a help to them, for when I come they immediately know all things and adore the Universal Father. Before such wise and philosophic ones die, they learn to renounce their senses, knowing that these are the enemies of their immortal souls.'

'I will not permit the evil senses to control the bodies of those who love me, nor will I allow evil emotions and evil thoughts to enter them. I become as a porter or doorkeeper, and shut out evil, protecting the wise from their own lower nature. But to the wicked, the envious and the covetous, I come not, for such cannot understand the mysteries of *Mind*; therefore, I am unwelcome. I leave them to the avenging demon that they are making in their own souls, for evil each day increases itself and torments man more sharply, and each evil deed adds to the evil deeds that are gone before until finally evil destroys itself. The punishment of desire is the agony of unfulfillment.'

Hermes bowed his head in thankfulness to the Great Dragon who had taught him so much, and begged to hear more concerning the ultimate of the human soul. So Poimandres resumed: 'At death the material body of man is returned to the elements from which it came, and the invisible divine man ascends to the source from whence he came, namely the *Eighth Sphere*. The evil passes to the dwelling place of the demon, and the senses, feelings, desires, and body passions return to their source, namely the Seven Governors, whose natures in the lower man destroy but in the invisible spiritual man give life."

These profound words from Hermes also echo the same wisdom that's found in the Emerald Tablets, which speaks to the divine and infinite nature of human consciousness. Many secrets are revealed in *The Vision of Hermes* if the reader studies their words carefully and separates the hidden symbols and metaphors. The story of Poimandres begins with Hermes finding himself wandering in a rocky and desolate place, where he allows himself to retreat into deep meditation and prayer. Following the secret instructions of the Mystery Schools, Hermes frees his higher consciousness from his physical body and is suddenly met by the celestial dragon known as Poimandres, who refers to themselves as the great mind and consciousness of the universe. Is this a reference back to the one true God, also known as the Prime Creator? This Great Dragon acts as the *final* gatekeeper of ascension for human beings, based on the moral rules of judgment that were laid down long ago. These moral rules, used to judge a human soul upon death, were closely followed by Osiris in Egypt, who eventually had to *assume* this role in the underworld.

Ordainers of Destinies and the Underworld

To me, it's clear that Marduk, Thoth, Ninmah, and Enki, along with their various incarnations, have played important roles in mankind's history. However, I will stress that some of them, such as Marduk and Enki, have *had* to play a more negative and deceptive role during certain time periods due to the laws of balance. Figure 6 below shows a serpent-dragon statue of Kukulkan at Chichen Itza, Mexico. Notice the striking similarities that can be found in these statues and murals throughout the Aztec, Toltec, and Maya cultures, which shows the strong connections they all had back to a common influence long ago.

Figure 6

Now you may be wondering what became of Enki's first-born son Marduk, and what was his specific role in our reality? Marduk was a second-generation god of the Anunna who rose in power to become the principle solar deity for the city of Babylon and was later known as Amun-Ra to the ancient Egyptians. Marduk's territory in the north was shared by Enlil and several of his sons, who were considered fierce rivals to him at the time. This resulted in the Assyrian Empire having its capital shared by both the cities of Babylon in the south (ruled by

Marduk) and Nineveh to the north (largely ruled by Enlil and his son Ninurta). This created intense conflict between the younger and older generation Anunnaki gods, who often created wars over controlling the regions of Mesopotamia, as well as to defend their status and prominence as supreme leaders. This should be seen as one of the major catalysts for why there has historically been so much conflict and turmoil between these cities.

Marduk assumed the role as the chief deity for the city of Babylonian where he was also known as Bel. Due to his powerful influence over the region and rivalry with Enlil, Marduk altered many of the ancient texts to portray himself as the supreme leader and hero to mankind. In fact, we find significant discrepancies between certain Babylonia versions of the Enuma Elish, where Marduk claims he created the human race, instead of his father Ea. This is an attempt by Marduk to re-write history in his favor. In many ways, this bitter rivalry seen between Marduk and Enlil represents a much deeper issue that exists between the Anunna, where the younger-generation was competing for power over the elders.

This rivalry is perhaps best seen in Egypt when Marduk assumed the role of Amun-Ra with the symbol of the falcon. This choice of a falcon is especially interesting if you consider that Enlil's symbol was an eagle, which is very similar to a falcon (except that the falcon is considered the *fastest* bird of all). During a time when these gods were fighting over supremacy of the region, the choice of a falcon is quite a fitting choice, to say the least. That's why Amun-Ra is symbolically shown with the head of a falcon; while Enlil, and those loyal to him, are historically shown associated with the eagle or one of its many variations. Despite this ongoing dispute between the Anunnaki over power, it seems a shaky alliance was later formed during the reorganization of the Roman Empire, where Marduk and Enlil assumed various roles within some of the Abrahamic religions.

At the height of its power, Babylon grew to become one of the largest cities on Earth, with a population of over 200,000 and a thriving trading center. The city was built equally divided on either side of the Euphrates River and bound by large defensive walls and gates. Babylon was ruled by a long dynasty of bloodline kings, including one of its most influential of all, known as Hammurabi. King Hammurabi came into power after his father died in 1712 BC, leaving him the throne.

Hammurabi built Babylon into a powerful military center of the region that would eventually merge and become the great strength of the Assyrian Empire. Hammurabi believed he was the divine and rightful king of Mesopotamia because he received direct instructions from the "gods" for how to govern over society. These instructions came in the form of a long list of moral laws and rules which became collectively known as the "Code of Hammurabi." The Code of Hammurabi represents one of the oldest and most significant cuneiform texts ever recovered in Babylon, yet despite this, most have never even heard of it.

The Code of Hammurabi is a large, 7.5-foot-tall stele with cuneiform writing that describes 282 laws to follow for bringing stability and morality to mankind. It became a guide that was followed by numerous kings and rulers and was eventually woven into the very fabric of our society. In the preface it states:

"When Anu, the Sublime King of the Anunnaki, and Bel, the lord of Heaven and earth, who decreed the fate of the land assigned to Marduk, the over-ruling son of Ea, god of righteousness, dominion over earthly man, that made him great among the Igigi. They called Babylon by his illustrious name, made it great on earth, and founded an everlasting kingdom in it, whose foundations are laid so solidly as those of heaven and earth. Then Anu and Bel called by name me, Hammurabi, the exalted prince, who feared God, to bring about the rule of righteousness in the land, to destroy the wicked and the evil-doers; so that the strong should not harm the weak, so that I should rule over the black-headed people like Shamash and enlighten the land, to further the well-being of mankind."

"When Marduk sent me to rule over men, to give the protection of right to the land, I did right and brought about the well-being of the oppressed."

This powerful quote not only mentions Anu by name but also explains the extensive influences that Bel (another name for Marduk) had on Babylon and much of the rest of Mesopotamia. This ancient text, along with the Sumerian King List, provides some of the most compelling evidence to show where the structure of our society originated from and how certain leaders were *chosen* to rule over the rest of people. This was done in order to gain new territory in their name, as well as to secure their prominence and legacy. Quotes like these also help to prove that the Anunnaki are real and have played a major role in our past. Notice how Marduk is mentioned as being the "lord of heaven and earth" instead of Enlil. Of all the younger generation Anunnaki gods, Marduk seems to play the most complicated role of all, assuming both sides of duality throughout human history. At times, Marduk spread wisdom and higher knowledge, while at other times it seems he promoted spiritual deceit and the use of black magic. That's why Bel is often associated with the practice of black magic in Babylon.

In order to provide balance, the Anunna were divided into playing different roles within our reality; some assuming a positive role, while others a negative, depending on the different time periods. Those who were assigned a negative role largely governed over the age of Aries and Pisces, ruling through a combination of war, promoting false religious doctrines, and by preying on our basic human urges. As stated previously in the book, this hatred and anger shared by some of the Anunnaki towards mankind stems from the jealousy and anger that arose long ago over the genetic gifts given to the human race, which many of them felt we didn't deserve in the first place.

Enlil was designated by Anu as the ruler of the higher realms of Earth, including the third dimension, and as such, oversaw both the activities of the Igigi, as well as the human race. Enlil's problem became how to maintain complete control over society since humans were created for the sole purpose of fulfilling the *physical* needs of the Anunna here. Enlil felt that mankind needed to be ruled with an iron fist to prevent uprisings and revolts, such as previously seen with the Igigi. The solution that Enlil and others came up with was to create chaos and confusion in our reality for the means of blocking mankind's spiritual ascension and trapping them in the physical world. That's why I continuously bring up the importance of understanding who we really are and why each one of us should seek to reach higher levels of consciousness.

The main reason that focusing society on money, war, and the illusion of the material world is so damaging to our conscious-evolutionary path, is due to the fact that our true identity is that of a multidimensional being, who is simply experiencing a physical reality here until we can grow on a spiritual level. By keeping humanity distracted by these clever illusions, they're forced to repeat this cycle of incarnation, eternally sacrificing their time and energy. Those are a few of the rules for how this "system" works, and why some have referred to our reality on Earth as a *prison*. But is it really a prison?

The ancient Gnostics claim that our primitive urges are the source of all misery on the planet and that an evil being; known as Jehovah in the Bible, continuously preys on them for the means of blocking our spiritual ascension. Since Enlil (who is playing the role of "God" in the story of Adam and Eve) doesn't want mankind to have the knowledge of higher consciousness, it should be no surprise then that he assumed this disruptive role in our reality. In Hebrew, Jehovah translates to mean "God" and is also considered to be the same being referred to as Yahweh. But is it really God? I would like to strongly point out at this time that Enlil is simply playing the role of God and is *not* actually affiliated with what I refer to as the "prime creator" or "great architect" of the universe. This gives credible evidence to not only suggest that Enlil is playing the role of God in the Bible, but also Jehovah, Yahweh, and Yaldabaoth.

In many ways, the Anunnaki could be considered nothing more than puppets for this powerful and all-seeing "prime" creator, who permits duality as a means of exploring all forms of free will and self-expression. In the end, despite the sheer abundance of evil that still rules our world, the specific laws that were woven into the design of the universe itself mean that the likely outcome will be one of growth and unity, rather than chaos and division. This hidden design can be seen throughout nature and has been echoed by past cultures and secret societies since the very beginning.

Mesopotamian cuneiform tablets, such as the Atrahasis, explain that Enlil was designated by Anu to become the all-mighty ruler and controller of the skies and upper dimensions of Earth. Because of that, his symbol became the eagle. This symbol was also shared by many of the Igigi (the Watchers), along with his son Ninurta, who later became associated with the Byzantine, double-headed eagle of the Roman Empire. These "gods of war" were responsible for the creation of powerful empires who systematically conquered the serpent-dragon civilizations of antiquity, nearly eradicating any evidence of their existence and polluting their teachings. That's how so many of our most important symbols that lead back to achieving higher states of consciousness and spirituality eventually became demonized and inverted over time.

This struggle of the eagle and serpent has been seen by many academics as merely symbolic, and not actually representing real beings. To me, this thought process represents a linear way of thinking, by ignoring the extensive evidence that exists showing the influence that these beings had on cultures across the world, who were sometimes separated by vast oceans and great distances. The chance that these similarities could have occurred naturally across all of these civilizations, with no outside intervention, is nearly impossible in my opinion, and in many ways illogical. The task of the objective researcher seeking the truth should always be to follow the evidence wherever it leads and to never allow predetermined conclusions to cloud one's judgment.

Enlil's half-brother and polar opposite was known as Ea to the Babylonians, and Enki to the Sumerians, which translates to mean: "Lord of the Earth." This title helps to show the particular role that he played here. Enki was represented by four primary symbols throughout history: the serpent-dragon, caduceus, fish, and the lifeforce of fresh water. The use of these symbols varied based on the time period, as well which specific role he was playing at the time. In ancient Mesopotamia, Enki was frequently portrayed as an aquatic fish-being known as Oannes. It's fascinating to learn that this same representation can also be seen in Mali, Africa with the Dogon tribe, and the beings they referred to as the "Nommo."

When one compares the detailed descriptions and unique fish symbolism shared by both Oannes and the Nommo, the evidence becomes almost impossible to refute. Clearly, both Oannes and the Nommo come from the influences of Ea. The historical comparisons and connections for Ea's influences in the past don't stop there though. When studying the significance of the religious Mitre Hat worn by the Pope and bishops in the Catholic Church, the similarities are uncanny and clearly point to its origins being linked back to Ea (Enki) and his role as Oannes during the days of Pisces. This all makes logical sense when you consider that one of Ea's roles and titles here was "Lord of the Waters," which is commonly shown in cylinder seals from Mesopotamia.

The use of numerous names and extensive symbols to represent the various influences and incarnations of these beings here is one of the major reasons why they've managed to remain secret and largely hidden from most of society. This is especially true when you consider all the tampering that's gone on with many of these ancient texts over time, as well as the likelihood that some of the Anunnaki left our physical realm long ago, as Thoth states in the Emerald Tablets. These challenges allowed the truth about the Anunna to become nearly lost to history and considered nothing more than a myth by most mainstream experts. That's why learning about this is so important to do right *now*; since we're living in a time period when this information is both free and readily accessible to most.

Of all the Anunnaki, the Sumerian gods of Enki and Ningishzida were the ones who were the most frequently associated with the symbols of the serpent and caduceus. This shows their dedication as eternal teachers for humanity, helping society reach higher states of consciousness and energy. Ningishzida, also called Gishzida, was assigned by Anu and Enlil to become a guardian and messenger for Enki in the underworld. That's the reason Ningishzida became associated with the role of a teacher and guide since both he and Enki took great pity on the unbalanced means by which our reality had been designed.

Evidence shows that Ningishzida was likely associated with the Atlantean priest Thoth, also called Tehuti in Egypt, who eventually assumed the role of Kukulkan and Quetzalcoatl in the America's, and later Hermes to the Greeks. All Hermetic writings are based on this great legacy left behind by "thought" (Thoth). That's why

Thoth was portrayed in ancient Egyptian and African societies with the head of an Ibis bird, who's commonly shown holding a writing utensil in one hand, symbolizing his eternal dedication as the patient teacher of mankind. Still, even with all of these glaring facts that reveal the positive influences that these serpent-dragon wisdom bringers had on cultures in the past, they would still become demonized as evil by the modern church. Eventually, most of society would also buy into this lie.

As I stated previously, most the Anunnaki became firmly split between two dualistic mentalities; with some focusing on wanting to assist mankind's progression, and others wanting to halt or slow it down. This distinction is necessary to point out, as Enki was assigned or even forced, into ruling the realm of the underworld as a means of maintaining *balance* there. That's why at times he had to assume a more negative or deceptive role in our reality. It's very important to understand that not all entities or beings that reside in the underworld are benevolent. In fact, according to the writings of the Emerald Tablets, most of them may be quite malevolent towards humanity, playing a significant role in much of the darkness and suffering seen throughout history.

Enki was assigned to the underworld to provide balance there, alongside his counterpart Nergal. This means that at *times* they've both had to play a negative and deceptive role to mankind. Some of the beings and entities that reside in the underworld can be conjured into our reality through the practice of black magic and blood sacrifice, which is why ancient texts describe how certain civilizations eventually became corrupted through its use, such as the Atlanteans, Babylonians, Aztec, and Maya. For those who are interested in learning the difference, a malevolent underworld spirit that was brought into the third dimension by a mortal priest was called an Utukku, while a benevolent spirit was known as a Lamassu. Much of this should begin to make sense when looking at the events of history and the confusion that surrounds the realm referred to as "hell."

Enki has been known by many names throughout history, including Ea, Enkig, Nudimmud, Oannes, or Ninsiku, and like Ningishzida, has played several important incarnation roles here. The most famous of these incarnations can be seen through the Greek god of Poseidon, as well as the Egyptian god Ptah. These various incarnations, names, and titles held by the Anunnaki can be accurately identified by studying the clues left behind in Mesopotamian cuneiform tablets and then separating out the various traits and symbols that each one of them carried. Quickly you will notice certain similarities and traits that are consistently shared by these beings in nearly every ancient culture. A good example of this can be found with the Greek god of Zeus (known as Enlil in Mesopotamia), where he's frequently portrayed in statues and murals with an eagle perched near or even on him. This type of objective reasoning can also be used to identify the specific influences they each had here in the past, by studying the symbolism found in flags and crests around the world.

As I have stated previously, both Enki and Enlil have played major roles in the rise and fall of human civilizations throughout history and should be seen as the primary players competing in this chess-match like game of controlling our reality here. The primary reason these two brothers became so divided is that each of them was given dual ownership of the realm of Earth, but neither shared any common mentalities or viewpoints. Due to these constant disagreements, Enki and Enlil (along with their numerous offspring commonly referred to as demigods), became separated into certain factions known as Enkiites or Enlilites. This division created the dualistic struggle that we still see today between the eagle and serpent. Now you may be asking yourself, what is the evidence that shows this struggle is real?

Cuneiform tablets state that thousands of years ago before these two Anunnaki brothers came to our realm, they were known as Ea and Enlil. At the time, Enki was referred to as Ea because he hadn't officially gained his title and status yet. The reason why I'm pointing out this distinction is to show that Enlil had already been given his official title before Enki was even assigned one. This shows that Enlil's royal status among the Anunna was higher than that of Enki. But why?

Evidence indicates that Enki's mother was likely a consort to his father, which meant that his status and ability to govern would always be overshadowed by his half-brother. This represents one of the main reasons why Enki's first-born son Marduk decided to play such a complicated role in our reality, as he realized that he would never be able to obtain full royal status within the Anunna due to his bloodline. Because of this, Marduk felt cheated out of his perceived destiny which is why he often considered himself the ultimate *sacrifice* and *savior* to mankind.

According to ancient Mesopotamian genealogy records, Enki was a son of the Anunnaki elder known as An, and his mother was called Nammu. Because Nammu was a consort of An, Enlil was considered next in line to rule the Anunnaki. Enlil also held a higher status and title than that of his half-brother Enki. This distinction in title is very important to understand, as it helps to explain both why human history has been ruled by so much control, war, and chaos under Enlil's reign, as well as the reason that there has been such a focus on protecting certain bloodlines here. It's by no means a coincidence then that many of the most powerful monarchies and elite family dynasties of the world *still* maintain this status quo here.

Due to Enlil's viewpoints of humanity, as well as his status within the council of the Anunnaki, it permitted him (and those loyal to him), to allow corruption, deception, and war to dominate our reality for thousands of years. As I stated before, this despicable act was done to block higher consciousness and spiritual ascension within mankind, as well as to attempt to play the role of gods. The only reason you're able to read these words now and not be at risk of torture or being burned at the stake is due to certain laws and freedoms that were finally enacted which have *temporarily* allowed this control system to lose its grip here. That's why this particular time period is so important.

These draconian decisions, which are based on a lack of compassion and severe mental psychosis, can be observed within many of the high-ranking military leaders and rulers of the past, who were often used as nothing more than pawns to promote a higher agenda. These kings and rulers were often promised ultimate power in exchange for their blind loyalty and dedication, which unknowingly led to the corruption of their souls in the end. That's the main reason why the symbol of the eagle (and phoenix) became embraced by so many warring empires of antiquity, while the serpent was eventually conquered and demonized.

To better understand which of the Anunnaki brothers influenced the various human cultures and empires across the planet, we need to follow their various names and symbols. The chart below contains a list of the possible names and incarnations that each one of these beings may have used over time. For those who are interested, an expanded version of this chart can be found towards the end of the book.

Enki and Enlil God Table

Human Civilizations	Ea	Enlil
Sumerian	Enki	Enlil
Akkadian	Ea	Ellil
Persian	Ahura Mazda	Angra Mainyu
Greek	Prometheus	Zeus
Roman	Neptune	Jupiter
Nordic	Loki	Thor
Slavic	Veles	Perun

I would like to strongly point out that evidence exists showing that Enki and Enlil likely played roles in other cultures as well, such as in India and the Americas; however, I didn't include them in the chart above due to conflicting information and a lack of specifics. My goal with this book is accuracy, so I will allow the reader to determine those influences for themselves.

The early aboriginal tribes of Australia referred to Enki as the "rainbow snake" and claimed that he inhabits the deep oceans and underworld realms of the planet. Enki was considered by them to be one of the greatest *creators* in all the universe. Pay close attention to that reference, as it also correlates with what Mesopotamian cuneiform tablets say about him. These conclusions make logical sense considering the fact that Enki is mentioned in the Atrahasis and Enuma Elish as being the creator of mankind, who was responsible for the specific design of the chakra centers in the human body. These chakra centers just so happen to perfectly reflect the vibrational energy of the visible light spectrum. That's why Enki is referred to as the "rainbow snake" by these aboriginal tribes of Australia since the term "rainbow" is both referencing his connection to the seven colors of the visible light spectrum, as well as "serpent," meaning his role as a wisdom bringer.

These inherent responsibilities given to Enki to manage the energy and soul incarnation cycles on the Earth is why he eventually became associated with Osiris in Egypt, due to his specific role as a balancer in the underworld, referred to as the Duat. Previously, Enki had assumed the role as a powerful pharaoh in Egypt before his brother Set (also known as Enlil), betrayed him and forced him to eternally rule in the underworld. This famous story is also echoed in the cuneiform tablet known as the Legend of Etana, along with other ancient text from around the world. Afterward, Horus; the son of Osiris and Isis, overthrew Set to take back control of

Egypt and rule as it's pharaoh. This clearly shows the significance that Egypt represented to the Anunna. The reason Egypt was so important to them was due to its specific location on the planet in relation to electromagnetic energy intersections, known as ley lines; which is why the great pyramids were built there in the first place.

The responsibilities given to Osiris in the underworld included the "weighing a human soul" after its death to determine final judgment. This is commonly depicted throughout history as a scale with a feather on one side, and heart on the other. If the human heart, represented through the pure karmic energy of that soul, weighs less than the feather, then it's allowed to ascend and leave this system of incarnation that was *created* here. To better understand how these various realms of Earth were divided and governed by the Anunnaki, along with the specific symbols they used to represent themselves, we turn to the ancient cuneiform tablet known as The Legend of Etana for answers.

Kingship, Lost Civilizations, and the Great Deluge

The Legend of Etana, also known as the Myth of Etana, is a set of Babylonian cuneiform tablets that provides an important historical perspective for the Post-Diluvian time period of Mesopotamia. Etana was considered to be the first king of Kish, which was a city located in the Fertile Crescent region of Iraq and Syria. According to the Sumerian King List, Kish was the first city on Earth that "kingship" was lowered to after the deluge. The reason the Legend of Etana is so important is that it provides a rare glimpse into the historical account of what occurred just *after* the events of the Epic of Atrahasis. This helps to fill in many of the gaps we still have for correctly understanding the timeline of the Younger Dryas period, and how it impacted ancient civilizations around the world. These cuneiform tablets represent one of the earliest references ever made for the serpent and eagle, as well as explaining how Enki and Enlil became associated with their particular roles within our reality.

The Legend of Etana was written in such a way as to hide its true meanings within clever parables and symbolic metaphors. This has caused it, and many other cuneiform tablets like it, to be largely ignored by most mainstream experts and academics, who consider them unimportant to history. However, this couldn't be further from the truth as you will soon read below.

Tablet 1 of the Legend of Etana begins with:

They planned a city
The gods laid its foundations
They planned the city [Kish]
The Igigi-gos founded its brickwork
"Let him be their (the people's) shepherd,
"Let Etana be their architect... "
The Great Anunnaki gods ordainers of destinies,
Sat taking their counsel concerning the land,
The creators of the four world regions, establishers of all physical form,
By command of all of them the Igigi gods
Ordained a festival for the people

No king did they establish, over the teeming peoples,
At that time no headdress had been assembled, nor crown,
Nor yet scepter had been set with lapis.
No throne daises whatsoever had been constructed,
Against the inhabited world they barred the gates...
The Igigi gods surrounded the city with ramparts
Ishtar came down from heaven to seek a shepherd,
And sought for a king everywhere.
Inanna came down from heaven to seek a shepherd,
And sought for a king everywhere.
Enlil examined the dais of Etana,
The man whom Ishtar steadfastly....
"She has constantly sought....
"Let kingship be established in the land,
Let the heart of Kish be joyful"

The first tablet of The Legend of Etana describes how the Anunnaki (ordainers of destinies) had to create a new world after the destruction of the old one by re-lowering kingship to the city of Kish. Etana was chosen to be its architect and ruler since he was part of the royal bloodline of kings that can be traced all the way back to before the time of Atrahasis and Ubara-Tutu. As we continue on with the second tablet of the Legend of Etana, pay close attention to the symbolic wording used in regards to the roles played by the serpent and eagle.

Tablet 2 of the Legend of Etana states:

"In the shade of the shrine a poplar was growing,
In its crown an eagle settled,
A serpent settled at its root.
Daily they watched the wind beasts.

The eagle made ready to speak, saying to the serpent,
"Come, let us make friendship,
Let us be comrades, you and I."
The serpent made ready to speak, saying to the eagle,
"If indeed you desire friendship, then let us swear a
mighty oath of Shamash.
"Come then, let us set forth and go up the high
mountain to hunt.
"Let us swear an oath by the netherworld."
Before Shamash the warrior they swore the oath.
"Whoever transgresses the limits of Shamash,
May Shamash deliver him as an offender into the
hands of the executioner.
After the eagle's children were grown big and were
flourishing,
The eagle's heart indeed plotted evil,
Evil his heart plotted indeed!
He set his thoughts upon eating his friend's young.
The eagle made ready to speak, saying to its children:
"I will eat the serpent's children,
then the serpent will be cast down,
and I will go up and dwell in heaven."
He descended and ate up the serpent's children,
In the evening of the same day,
The serpent came, bearing his burden,
He looked down, his children were gone!
The eagle had gouged the ground with his talon,
The cloud of dust from the sky darkened the sky..."

According to the second tablet of the Legend of Etana, the serpent is betrayed by the eagle, through his evil trickery and cast down to eternally rule the underworld. At the same time, the eagle travels up to "dwell in heaven." To me these are clear references back to the story of the serpent god of Enki, who are forced to permanently rule in the underworld, also called the Duat or abzu. At the same time, Enlil, who is represented by the eagle, rules in the higher dimensions of "heaven" where he presides over the physical world. This evidence not only supports the internal conflict and division that developed within the Anunna, but also shows that these beings became so advanced that they developed the ability to become non-corporeal, meaning that they could exist without a physical body, on an interdimensional level.

Just as the Atrahasis and Epic of Gilgamesh represent the accounts of the early kings of Mesopotamia, The Legend of Etana is also written from the perspective of a king named Etana, who are mentioned in the Sumerian King List as ruling over the city of Kish. Kish is referenced in the Sumerian King List as being the first city on Earth where kingship was re-lowered to after the deluge swept over. Like Atrahasis, King Etana represents one of the great kings of Sumer, but more specifically he was part of what's known as the Postdiluvian time period (meaning after the flood).

These Pre-Diluvian and Postdiluvian civilizations of Mesopotamia are very important to understand and distinguish because they represent two distinct time periods that are separated by great catastrophes. This is why so little evidence remains today from the Pre-Diluvian cities of Eridu, Bad-tibira, Larag, and

Shuruppak, which became buried and nearly lost to history. In order to more clearly understand these different time periods of the past and the events that led up to the cataclysms at the end of the last ice age, we have to review the climate data from ice-core samples from Greenland, geologic evidence from North America, and cuneiform tablets from Mesopotamia.

Ancient texts, pyramids, and megalithic ruins provide compelling evidence to show that more than 10,000 years ago, advanced civilizations once thrived from the region of Peru and Bolivia, across the ocean to Lebanon, Jordon, Mesopotamia, India, and Egypt, that all disappeared without warning from great catastrophes that occurred across the planet. To fully understand the chronological timeline of these lost civilizations that disappeared between 10,000 and 12,800 years ago, we must study the evidence that's echoed by nearly every major culture of the past.

These events, referred to collectively as the cataclysms of the Younger Dryas, wiped away much of what existed before, causing a reset button on human civilizations. This gave rise to the Postdiluvian kingdoms of Mesopotamia, including Uruk, Ur, or Kish. The most important thing to understand with these events is that they were caused by a combination of several apocalyptic disasters that all occurred in a relatively short time period, including a destructive solar outburst or comet strike, large earthquakes and tsunamis, and abrupt climate change, which led to a rapid melting of the ice caps. As impossible as that may sound to some, there is extensive evidence that exists all around the world that supports these claims. Allow me to explain.

Geologic anomalies seen in the landscapes of

Montana, Oregon, and Washington provide compelling evidence to indicate that during the Younger Dryas, rapid melting of the northern ice cap occurred, leading to colossal flooding and mass extinctions of megafauna in the region. Just imagine for a moment that you were alive during this event and lived just south of the Canadian border where there was an ice cap that was 1-2 miles deep just to your north. You would have witnessed thousands of square miles of ice that suddenly, without warning, melted, leading to a torrent of water, ice, and mud across the entire area. The event that caused this disaster was so extreme that it altered the climate of the planet for thousands of years.

When you begin to account for the disappearance of so many civilizations from the past, as well as the large extinction seen with many of the land animals of the region, such as the wooly mammoth and saber-toothed tiger, it all begins to correlate and make logical sense. That's why we see such a stark contrast between the advanced Pre-Diluvian civilizations and the less developed Postdiluvian civilizations. Evidence to support this theory can be found when studying each one of these Pre-Diluvian sites around the world, where you see extreme scarring and burning that occurred on many of the megalithic structures. In the future, this lost time period in history will likely be one of the most heavily studied areas of all.

The information found within the Atrahasis, Sumerian King List, and Eridu Genesis represent some of the most comprehensive and important evidence that exists to explain these disastrous events that occurred long ago. Ancient religions and cultures all over the planet have also told nearly the same story. The Atrahasis cuneiform tablets contain both the creation story of mankind, as well as the deluge, making them unique among Mesopotamian writings. It explains that the royal council of Anunna decided that humans were being too "loud" and decided to created diseases, plagues, and finally, a great flood to cleanse the planet. The tablet is called the "Epic of Atrahasis" because it represents his viewpoint of the events that occurred during this particular time period, which gives credibility for this information, considering that he is mentioned in the Sumerian King List as being alive *before* the flood.

The Atrahasis was first discovered in the Ashurbanipal Library of Nineveh in 1849. Since then other versions have surfaced from Babylon and Sippar, all of which echo nearly the same story. Atrahasis was a son of Ubara-Tutu, one of the early kings of the city of Shuruppak, who handed over power to his son just before the deluge occurred. This transition of power is well documented in the cuneiform tablets known as the Instructions of Shuruppak, where Atrahasis is known by one of his alternate names of Ziusudra (the flood hero).

According to Ziusudra, he was warned about the incoming disaster because he was considered one of the direct descendants of Enki himself, who wanted his bloodline to be protected in order to repopulate the Earth after the deluge. The tablets of the Atrahasis not only provide important historical information about these violent events that occurred at the end of the last ice age but also who these *rulers of our reality* really are, as discussed in the Nag Hammadi Scriptures.

To better understand how exactly an ancient global civilization could have been destroyed and nearly lost to time, we'll continue with the Atrahasis, specifically reading from tablets two and three.

Tablet 2 of the Atrahasis states:

600 years, less than 600 passed
The country became too wide, the people too numerous
Enlil grew restless at their racket, listening to their noise.
He addressed the great gods,
"The noise of mankind has become too much,
I am losing sleep over their racket.
Give the order that suruppu-disease shall break out.
Cut off food supplies to the people!
Let the vegetation be too scant for their hunger!"

When the sixth year arrived,
Only one or two households were left.
The people's looks were changed by starvation.
Their faces were covered in scabs like malt.
They stayed alive by holding onto life.

Enlil became furious and fetched Enki
"We, the great Anunna, all of us
Agreed together on a plan.
Anu and Adad were to guard above,
I, Enlil was to guard the Earth below.
Where you went (*Enki*), you were to undue the chain and set us free.

You were in charge of control and holding the balance.

But instead you gave wisdom and knowledge to the
people.
Your creations have become too numerous and despoiled
the Earth.

You imposed your loads on man,
You bestowed noise on mankind,
You slaughtered a god together with his intelligence,
Let us make far-sighted Enki swear an oath to the end,
To create a flood on Earth to wipe away all of life."

Enki spoke to his brother gods,
"Why should you make me swear an oath?
Why should I use my power against the people?
That is Enlil's kind of work!

Tablet 3 of the Atrahasis states:

There was once one named Atrahasis
whose ear was open to his god Enki.
He would speak with his god
And his god would speak with him.

Enki made his voice heard to Atrahasis;
Dismantle the house, build a boat,
Reject possessions, and save living things.
The boat you will build,
Roof it like the Apsu,
So that the sun cannot see inside it.
Make upper decks and lower decks. The tackle must be
very strong,

The bitumen strong, to give strength."

Atrahasis received the message and gathered the elders.
Everything was completed as instructed,
Atrahasis put all of his family on board.
Then the face of the weather changed.
Rain bellowed from the clouds,
Bitumen was brought to seal the door.

The winds were raging as Atrahasis cut the rope to
release the boat.
Then the flood came and no one could see anyone else,
They could not be recognized in the catastrophe.
The Flood roared like a bull,
Like a wild ass screaming, the winds howled
The darkness was total, there was no sun.
For seven days and seven nights
The torrent, storm and flood came on.

The goddess Mami watched and wept
"However could I, in the assembly of the gods,
Have ordered such destruction on them?"

Nintu was wailing;
"I have seen, and wept over them!
Shall I ever finish weeping for them?"

After the noise of the flood had subsided,
The warrior Enlil spotted the boat of Atrahasis.
He was furious!

"We the great Anunna, all of us
Agreed together on an oath!

No form of life should have escaped!
How did any man survive the catastrophe?"

Anu made his voice heard and spoke to the warrior
Enlil,
"Who but Enki would do this?"

Enki made his voice heard and spoke to the great gods,
"I did it, in defiance of you!
I made sure life was preserved.
Exact your punishment from the sinner, and whoever
contradicts your order."

The details provided within the Atrahasis about this devastating flood that occurred on Earth more than 10,000 years ago can be extremely difficult to accept and stomach at times. The idea that humans nearly went extinct due to starvation, plagues, and a devastating catastrophe brought on by the very beings who helped to create us, is mind-blowing to consider. Sadly, despite the sheer importance of what's contained within the tablets of the Atrahasis, most of society, and the larger academic community, still consider it nothing more than a myth.

This is astonishing to me considering that this ancient text not only mentions the Anunna directly by name but provides detailed information about the great deluge, as well as the origin story of mankind. In the next chapter, I will be discussing in much greater detail the potential reasons for why these disasters occurred during the last ice age, as well as the mysteries that still surround the outer Solar System.

Now let's go deeper into the dualistic nature and

specific symbolism used by these archons, who are collectively known as the Anunnaki by the Sumerians, or fallen angels in some religions. As I stated previously, one of the most important aspects to incorporate and understand about the events of history, is that the Council of Twelve, made up of the royal Anunna, became greatly divided amongst two competing factions: with one side wanting to assist and help humanity, and the other wanting to trap us in eternal bondage through chaos and the illusion of the material world.

This "war in heaven" has been mentioned throughout history, but the most notable reference can be found in *The Book of Revelation,* where it states that the "angels," led by Archangel Michael, go to war against those led by "the dragon," identified as the devil or Satan, who are eventually defeated and cast down to Earth. This same story is also echoed by *The Legend of Etana*, as well as several other cuneiform tablets from Mesopotamia, which helps to support its authenticity.

To me, this iconic story is clearly referencing Enki and Ningishzida being forced to rule in the underworld, while Enlil (and those loyal to him), rule over heaven and control the physical realm of Earth. Quickly you begin to see that not only are these stories based on historical truth, but they also help to explain how our reality ended up favoring these malevolent "heroes" of antiquity.

The Eagle versus the Serpent

One of the most enlightening moments of my life occurred while studying the specific symbolism found within many of the statues, murals, flags, and crests of the past cultures and empires of the planet and discovering the sheer scope and extent for how often the eagle and serpent were shown. From the Americas to the Sumerian and Egyptian civilizations, all the way through the Roman, Spanish, Slavic, German, Japanese, and Russian Empires, the eagle and serpent have played a major role throughout each of their histories.

However, the objective researcher will quickly realize that the eagle eventually became the dominant symbol in nearly every one of these cultures. This is also reflected in the specific mentality seen with most of their leaders. This correlation is by no means a coincidence and can be easily noticed if one looks at ancient history closely enough. Unfortunately, due to the level of conditioning and misinformation that's occurred, most are unaware of these important connections.

One of the best examples that can still be seen today to show the corruption by the eagle is found with the United States of America, or what I refer to as the "Empire of the United States." As unpopular as this may be to some, we can't ignore facts any longer simply because it's difficult to accept. Much like the Aztec and Maya cultures of Mexico eventually became dominated by a war-conquering mentality, so too did the United States.

It's important to understand though that in all three of these cases, these societies weren't originally founded with these principles, and only through the means of outside influences did they succumb to this fate. For instance, the early Founding Fathers of the United States intended to create a free and open nation, which was protected by the rules of free speech through the act of the Constitution. It wasn't until the time period of WW2 (and more specifically Operation Paperclip), when the US would eventually become infiltrated and corrupted by both Nazi loyalists and certain secret societies, such as the Illuminati. Previous to that, the banking families of the Rothschilds had already begun taking over and privatizing the Federal Reserve due to debt. Famous presidents such as Truman, Eisenhower, and JFK extensively warned the public about this hostile takeover that was occurring, which they called: "The Military Industrial Complex."

In 1945, just as WW2 was nearing its end and Nazi scientists were being rounded up and imprisoned, the United States decided that the most effective means of beating the Soviet Union and become the dominant power of the world, would be to "temporarily employ" as many of these Nazi scientists as possible. The reason for this was because they learned that these scientists had developed advanced technologies that they wanted to acquire and use. These Nazi scientists were not only extremely intelligent but were known as practicing Eugenicists, which meant that they believed that certain "supreme" races should rule the world. This secret operation by the US military was known as Operation Paperclip, which together with the privatization of the Federal Reserve by the Rothschild Central Bank, sealed the fate of the United States under its control.

Over time, the information describing both the events of the past, as well as the meanings behind these important ancient symbols, have been greatly tampered with and inverted to the point where they no longer represent the truth. The best example of this can be seen through how a majority of society views the symbols of the eagle and serpent. To most, the symbol of the eagle represents freedom and sovereignty, while the serpent represents deception or evil. As I have previously explained, the evidence clearly points to their meanings representing the opposite of what we've been taught. This information can be difficult for many to reintegrate into their thought process, due to the level of false conditioning that has occurred with these symbols for so long. That's the reason why I bring up this example so often.

When studying the various flags, coat of arms, and crests of many of the empires and conquering nations of history, a startling picture begins to emerge to show the level of domination that the eagle has achieved in each one of them. Nearly every country on the planet that has at one time, or still currently, portrays an eagle or phoenix on its flag or crest almost always became based on war and the conquering of other nations. This is not merely a coincidence, but a telltale sign back to the truth of who influenced them. The following is a compilation of *some* of the countries that have shown, or still show, an eagle or phoenix on their flag, coat of arms, or crest: Albania, Austria, Colombia, Czech Republic, Egypt, England, France, Germany, Iraq, Libya, Mexico, Moldova, Montenegro, Philippines, Poland, Romania, Russia, Serbia, Spain, United Arab Emirates, the United States, and Yemen.

It's important to point out that not all the counties mentioned above are still actively engaged in empire building or war. However, this list still provides a historical viewpoint to show the degree to which the eagle has managed to infiltrate and corrupt these governments over time. A good example to show this can be seen with the secret society known as the Freemasons, of which many of the Founding Fathers of the United States were all members.

The Freemasons represent one of the *last* global secret societies that had historically protected the ancient knowledge of sacred geometry and esoteric wisdom from antiquity. But like many of these organized groups and societies, they were eventually infiltrated and corrupted by those affiliated with the eagle. Evidence for this can be easily seen through the evolution of the emblem worn by the 33 Degree Masons, which eventually came to portray the symbol of the double-headed Byzantine eagle. This infiltration and corruption was accomplished by the rival secret society known as the Bavarian Illuminati, whose members include the Rothschild and Rockefeller families. These secret societies and elite families managed to seize control of most of the world's governments through infiltration and the power of the Central Bank.

The Anunnaki are considered by many to be the master architects behind the structure of our reality, designing the specific laws and moral rules that govern all of society. This kingship model goes far beyond just representing a set of laws and rules though, but defines *how* humans perceive their existence in the physical world, as well as in the universe. Therefore, if a society is dominated by war, ignorance, and fear, then they'll be locked in their lowest form of consciousness and will be trapped in a state of energy that they *don't* belong in. That's how these tactics became such an effective tool for controlling mankind without their awareness of it. That hidden design, aimed at suppressing human consciousness and spiritual growth, is evidence to show who *still* controls our reality today. After all, no human would ever be able to design such a perfect system.

The ancient symbol of the eagle, along with its many variations, can be traced all the way back to the beginning of when kingship was first "lowered" down to The Fertile Crescent of Mesopotamia, which gave rise to the Sumerian, Babylonian, Akkadian, and Assyrian civilizations. This specific model of rulership that was lowered to Mesopotamia, which later spread throughout the world, is almost always represented through a royal bloodline-kingship structure, based around hierarchical control, fear, and military strength.

This specific mentality of governing has changed little over time and is still largely in place even today. But why is that the case? Many of the mainstream academics and historians would argue that this is simply due to the natural course of our evolving human nature and is *not* connected back to any outside influences. So, what is the truth? The answer to that question is complicated, so please allow me to explain.

In most cases, humans will avoid conflict at all costs, unless they're continuously provoked or even forced into a violent mentality from continuous conditioning. Over the course of human history, it's clear that violence and war have ruled society since the very beginning. On the surface, this seems to define our true nature. But does it really? What I've come to conclude is this: war is indicative of a primitive and unevolved state of a being, and thus, has been used as a tool by some the Anunnaki and certain secret societies to prevent mankind's spiritual growth and conscious ascension. This social conditioning paradigm has occurred for so long that it's often been falsely associated with being a normal part of our human nature when it's really quite the opposite. Those faulty conclusions are often derived from ignorance and simplistic thinking, and don't account for outside influences and the ability to grasp the "bigger picture." A good example to show this can be seen with many of the isolated tribes found in the Amazon or remote Pacific islands, who will avoid war and conflict at all costs and have no interest in conquering others.

So, the most important question to ask is, if war and empire building are based on nothing more than basic human nature, then why aren't these indigenous tribes of the Amazon and remote Pacific islands seeking to conquer the entire region and the rest of the world? The reason is due to their isolated locations, which were far enough away as to not be as influenced by these warmongers of the past. Many of these remote cultures live in almost total harmony with nature and often want nothing more than to be left alone in peace and quiet. To me, this represents the *true* nature and mentality of most humans. Instead of understanding the fundamentals of balance and harmony with Mother Earth, the human race has been ruled by violence, greed, and ignorance for hundreds of generations.

When objectively studying the identity of who the various rulers and leaders of history were, you find out that many of them were part of specific bloodlines and secret societies, whose ancestors can be traced all the way back to the kings of Mesopotamia. That's why so many of these royal dynasty families that are still around today are so focused on maintaining these bloodlines, as very little has actually changed from antiquity.

Many of these bloodlines kings and elites believe they are superior to the rest of humanity, and because of that, use war to both control populations and to gain status and power over one other. The origins of this mentality can be understood through the important concept of "as above so below." According to Sumerian cuneiform records, long ago, the supreme ruler the Anunnaki (known as Anu) designated each of his various sons and daughters to control certain territories on the planet. Enlil and Ninurta were given ownership of most of the territory of Mesopotamia, including much of Asia Minor, while Enki and Marduk were given Africa, India, and eastern Asia.

It's by no means a coincidence then that the largest empires of the world originated out of the regions ruled by Enlil and Ninurta, such as the Assyrian, Hittite, Roman, and Ottoman Empires. To me, it's clear that the goal of this chess-match like game being played here by the Anunna is to either create powerful empires to further their legacy or infiltrate and corrupt existing ones for the means of gaining supremacy over each other. To better understand the full story of this "war in the heavens" between the Anunnaki, we must travel back more than 12,000 years ago to the time of Atlantis.

Ancient records indicate that at one time, there existed a sophisticated lost civilization known as Atlantis, which was located somewhere off the coast of Morocco or in the western part of Africa. What made Atlantis so important and unique was not merely its apparent physical beauty and sacred-geometric design, but the level of consciousness that its citizens had achieved. This was by no means an accident, as Atlantis was created and ruled over by a long line of benevolent kings; this included its founder Poseidon, who we know was connected to or may have even been an incarnation of Enki himself.

Because of the ongoing struggle that was occurring in "heaven," great conflict arose between the rival brothers of Enki and Enlil over the future of Atlantis. Due to the practice of black magic and other negative influences by some of the Anunnaki, a segment of its population became morally corrupted and was divided amongst two competing factions within society. Over time, this led to the eventual downfall of this great civilization, causing Thoth and others to leave the region. Combined with both the natural disasters of the Younger Dryas, as well as the misuse of advanced technologies, all of Atlantis was destroyed and swallowed up by the Atlantic Ocean.

The details of the deluge discussed within cuneiform tablets from Mesopotamia, as well as evidence recorded in North America and Greenland, provides compelling data to help explain why so many different animals went extinct at the end of the last ice age. The reason this extinction was so severe was due to the combination of several catastrophes that all occurred in a relatively short time period, which caused a rapid end of the last ice age, and dramatic temperature, precipitation, and ocean level fluctuations. This led to the destruction of an advanced, global civilization that was existed on the Earth which became nothing more than a myth by society. The more information that you uncover about the past, the more you find that it's all closely linked and connected.

Before Atlantis was destroyed, a segment of its population managed to leave and attempted to restart their civilization in locations such as Gobekli Tepe in Turkey, along the Nile River in Egypt, and in parts of the Americas. This is the underlying reason why today we find megalithic ruins in each of these locations that display sophisticated building techniques that would have been *impossible* to create using primitive or bronze-age tools. According to the Emerald Tablets, Thoth and his trusted priests and masons left Atlantis and decided to settle in the land of Khem (in the region today referred to as Egypt), due to its proximity to energy convergence centers and the availability of water for agriculture. Thoth then states that *he* created the pyramids of Giza, as well as the civilizations of Egypt, to protect the serpent-dragon knowledge of Atlantis so that its legacy could be preserved.

The precise mathematical designs and harmonic frequencies found within the Great Pyramid of Giza were created for the means of utilizing and harnessing the abundant electromagnetic energy found near the convergence of these energy centers on the Earth, known as ley lines. That's why the pyramids and megalithic temples located around the world were specifically built in the locations that they were. Along with these wonders, the ancient civilizations of Khem also created extensive tunnel systems underneath Giza to house the important knowledge from Atlantis, which was stored deep underground in secure libraries such as the famous Halls of Records. These libraries were designed to survive for thousands of years to preserve this vital information.

The vast knowledge and technological sophistication seen within the pyramids of Giza and the temples at Karnak, strongly indicate that the Pre-Dynastic Egyptians were influenced long ago by Thoth and his enlightened priests from Atlantis. In order to better understand the influences and significance of the eagle and serpent symbolism in the past, we'll need to temporarily jump forward to the time period of the Roman Empire.

However, I'll be returning to Thoth and his role in the Maya and Aztec civilizations later in the chapter.

Following the rise and fall of empires throughout human history, few could rival the sheer military strength and vast territory held by the Romans. As with other civilizations who were historically based around conquering and war, such as the Nazis or Spanish Empire, the Romans also used the symbol of the eagle on nearly all of its flags and banners and considered it to be their official standard. The Romans referred to this important symbol as the Aquila, which can be seen below in Figure 7.

Figure 7

In Latin, the word "Aquila" meant "eagle," which was used as the standard of the Roman Legion in war. During these battles, the legionary who carried the standard was known as an aquilifer, or eagle-bearer, whose sole responsibility was dedicated to its protection, at any cost. A missing Aquila standard was considered a serious loss to the Romans and they often went to great lengths to obtain them again. This meant sometimes searching for years to reacquire it, and often at the cost of many lives. It should become clear when looking at the extensive lengths that the Romans were willing to go to protect and secure the Aquila that the symbol of the eagle represented far more than simply military strength and order to them. This blind mentality and sheer dedication towards protecting the image of the eagle is a clear signal back to who really controlled these empires.

The Roman Empire was ruled through a combination of fear, propaganda, and violent entertainment which was done to condition its citizens to support the military endeavors of the empire, as well as to forget the larger problems that plagued their society. This was accomplished through coliseum "games" where barbaric and bloody battles were regularly displayed in front of its citizens who eagerly cheered them on. In more modern times, some would consider this form of entertainment as antiquated and merely a remnant of the past; yet today, looking all around us we can still find this watered-down version in many violent sporting events, which are then broadcast to the world.

This type of conditioning is best seen with the United States of America, where most of its citizens have been conditioned to support global military action, while at the same time believing their country represents sovereignty and freedom. By now, it should become apparent to the objective observer, regardless of where they may live, that the influences of the eagle have corrupted much of our planet. Always remember that actions speak louder than words, and proud patriotism shouldn't be used as an excuse to ignore obvious facts. That's one of the main reasons why some of the early Founding Fathers of the U.S originally wanted a turkey as the official emblem, instead of an eagle. In the end, we should always remember that we live on the Earth, and the use of artificial boundaries, war, and clever conditioning can only rule our conscious awareness for so long. One day in the future, humanity will realize that collaboration and unity are far more effective towards the collective growth of our society rather than competition against one another. So now you may be asking yourself the important question of, who were these secret rulers behind the Roman Empire?

Evidence shows that the Sumerian gods of Enlil and his son Ninurta were likely the great puppet masters behind the Roman Empire. Ninurta's symbol was the double-headed Byzantine eagle, which represented the Empire's dominance over both the east and west and considered a warning to all of those who opposed him. The symbol of the double-headed eagle can also be found throughout secret societies and religions across the world, showing the extensive means by which Ninurta managed to infiltrate and corrupt them. A good example of this can be seen with the emblem worn by the 33 Degree Masons that clearly portrays the double-headed eagle on it. The origins of the double-headed eagle can be traced back to the rise of the Byzantine Empire, a name used to specifically reference the Eastern Roman Empire, which was later renamed to the Holy Roman Empire.

Records indicate that Ninurta's father Enlil likely played the role of "God" in both the Hebrew Bible, as well as the New Testament, and was directly connected to the Rothschild family dynasty and the rise of Zionism. Together with his son Ninurta, they became powerful figures within both the Roman Empire, as well as in Christianity, leading to hundreds of years of bloody religious wars and pagan cleansing. At the same time, evidence shows that Marduk (Enki's first-born son), was also competing for power and supremacy, and likely played a deceptive role during this dark time period in human history as well. The reason this was allowed to occur is due to the negative polarity that ruled the Zodiac Age of Pisces. In fact, there are even early depictions of the symbol of the eagle that can still be found in some churches in Europe.

By retracing the events of history, we can pinpoint precisely when this hostile takeover of religion occurred. This takeover led to many of the Gnostic and Sumerian stories from the past being cleverly tampered with and significantly altered. This was done primarily for two reasons. First, to block off the path of spiritual ascension within society; and second, to venerate and worship these cruel gods of war and blood sacrifice. It seems that even Marduk (through one of his later incarnations), also became one of the deceivers within Christianity, since he felt that he represented the ultimate *sacrifice* to mankind. That's why the phrase "amen" can be traced back to him. Let's review the evidence that supports these conclusions.

Now it may seem peculiar to some that Marduk would assume a deceptive role in religion, especially considering that he provided enlightenment to ancient cultures in Egypt during his incarnation as Amun-Ra. The reason for this was due to the dualistic role that he played throughout history, for the means of both becoming the supreme god of the Anunnaki, as well as the savior of mankind. Before we further discuss the details of Marduk's role in Christianity, we need to first review the timeline for the Roman Empire and the rise of the double-headed Byzantine eagle.

In 313 AD, the Roman Emperor Constantine 1st decreed that Christianity would become the official religion of the empire. This may seem like a strange move to those who have studied the events of the past, especially considering that just prior to this decision the Roman Empire was brutally persecuting anyone who *was* a Christian. After hundreds, if not thousands of lives had been lost due this crackdown on religion, you may be wondering, why the sudden change of heart? The answer can be found by understanding the decisions made by Constantine 1st, as well as those who influenced him.

In 330 AD, as the Roman Empire lay in pieces and was on the brink of collapse, emperor Constantine 1st strategically moved all of his forces and military strength to a new capital in northern Turkey that he called Constantinople, which was dedicated in honor of his "greatness." In the newly constructed capital of Constantinople, the Roman Empire was reorganized into what became known as the Holy Roman Empire, which marked a critical moment in history when Christianity became infiltrated and corrupted. This disastrous outcome of power and control would eventually lead to the systematic destruction of countless cuneiform tablets and rare artifacts, along with the targeted eradication of any pagan societies that still practiced the forbidden serpent-dragon teachings from antiquity.

Over time, the sheer level of control and influence that the Holy Roman Empire had was seen through the corruption of countless governments and societies around the world, leading them to become war based economies who focused on the conquering of other regions and the acquisition of natural resources. This destructive mentality can be traced all the way back through history to the lowering of kingship in Mesopotamia thousands of years ago and provides further evidence to show who really influenced these empires. Now with large armies at their disposal, and a dangerous ideology fueling their motives, the Holy Roman Empire and Christian church began a massive cleanse aimed at ridding the ancient Gnostic and Druid people from the planet. This was an attempt to destroy the teachings and wisdom passed down by the early Egyptian and Atlantean cultures from the past. Now you may be wondering, what exactly happened to Thoth and the serpent-dragon civilizations of the Americas?

In order to grasp the destructive and long-term impacts that the crusades of the Spanish had on the indigenous people of North and South America, we'll first need to return to the time period when Thoth was still in Egypt, more than 10,000 years ago. During the end of his reign in Egypt, Amun-Ra seized control of the region and forced Thoth to retreat westward into Mexico and eventually the Americas. Amun-Ra then changed the calendar from a lunar to a solar one, which still remains to this day. All of this begins to make sense if you consider that Thoth became known as the moon god, while Amun-Ra took on the role of the sun god.

After Thoth left Egypt, he traveled west with his trusted temple priests and masons where he helped to establish the Inca, Olmec, Aztec, and Maya civilizations. This was an attempt by him to create a new Atlantis for the purpose of protecting its important wisdom. That's why in Tula, Mexico we find large monolithic statues that are called the "Atlantean Warriors." At first, it succeeded, as grand civilizations were created there that practiced the lost teachings from Atlantis to reach higher states of consciousness and achieve harmony and balance. Unfortunately, though, the cataclysms of the Younger Dryas destroyed many of these civilizations, and those who attempted to re-build afterward lacked the knowledge of their elders. That's why in virtually *all* these ancient megalithic sites, we find the most sophisticated building techniques on the lowest levels.

What we commonly refer to as the Inca, Aztec, Maya, and Toltec are actually their ancestors from earlier cultures. To complicate things even further, these cultures who attempted to re-build the megalithic temples of their elders were still seen as a threat to both the Christian church, as well as to some of the Anunnaki, who were also competing for supremacy in the region. Are you confused yet? Let's just say the true history of the Americas is incredibly complicated.

I would like to strongly point out that *none* of these beings or entities, including Thoth, are the true "God" or prime creator of the universe. However, I will stress that the reason I discuss and defend some of these wisdom bringers so often, is that I believe they are essentially trying to fix the unbalance that was caused here long ago. If an individual objectively investigates the details of what occurred in history, they begin to see that much of the turmoil and chaos that engulfed the planet was due to the rift that developed between these powerful beings. This should be viewed as the main catalyst behind the ancient struggle of the eagle and serpent, which continues to this day.

On the surface, it seems apparent that the gods of the eagle have won here, but for how long? Only time will tell. The extensive influences from the serpent-dragon teachers of the past can be seen throughout the indigenous cultures of the Americas. From the Hopi and Puebloan people of the United States to the Aztec, Toltec, and Maya of Mexico, all the way to the Inca of South America, their great legacy still lives on through the sacred texts, statues, and ancient temples they helped to create. In the end, the true purpose for creating these civilizations of Americas was done for the means of resurrecting what had been lost from the destruction of Atlantis, centuries before. Unfortunately, though, it failed to succeed. Let's dig into why.

One of the most frequent misconceptions that I come across regarding the progression and evolution of these indigenous cultures of the Americas, is that they were all corrupted by blood sacrifice and war by the influences of Kukulkan and Quetzalcoatl. However, the evidence clearly shows that these wisdom bringers were fiercely *opposed* to these practices. So, you may be wondering then, who, or what was it that corrupted them? Seeing how the legacy and symbols carried by Thoth and Enki were eventually demonized by the church, as well as by many of the Anunnaki themselves, evidence supports the theory that they weren't the ones who were primarily responsible. That's just the tip of the iceberg though.

This chess-match like game to dominate our world

(being fought over between Enlil, Nergal, Ninurta, and Marduk), meant that they were willing to undertake whatever means were necessary to reign supreme. The path of blood sacrifice and war that was eventually followed by the Maya and Aztec civilizations can be explained by understanding what occurred in history with the absence of Kukulkan and Quetzalcoatl, who eventually had to leave these civilizations in order to move on to other parts of the world.

Over time, their absence created panic and desperation among many of these cultures, as the climate was rapidly changing, and the weather patterns had become unpredictable. Eventually, malevolent beings who were represented through the symbol of the eagle and jaguar took advantage of the fragile situation in the Americas, and pretended to be the returning plumed serpent god(s) of Kukulkan/Quetzalcoatl.

These malevolent beings and deities managed to convince the leaders of the Aztec and Maya cultures to focus on war and practice blood sacrifice. This led them down a dark road of unbalance and corruption. Just as seen throughout history, many of these past kings and rulers (such as Moctezuma), became used as nothing more than puppets to carry out unspeakable acts of violence against their citizens. According to ancient Maya codices, one of the main influences of this madness seems to revolve around the entity known as God L, who is responsible for a large amount of the suffering and blood sacrifice seen within the Maya. It's important to point out that many of these gods and deities worshipped by the Maya and Aztec were commonly represented by letters, such as God D or God L, and were almost always portrayed as fighting amongst one another. So you may be wondering, who exactly was God L?

Evidence shows that the Maya deity known as God L is most closely associated with the Mesopotamian underworld ruler named Nergal, who was a son of Enlil and consort to Ereshkigal. Nergal was also called Erra or Irra and was considered an underworld god of both death and warfare. This struggle for control among the Anunna in these civilizations of the Americas begins to make sense when you consider the fact that Nergal and others played the negative roles of duality in the underworld, while Enki and Ningishzida mostly played positive roles.

In the Maya and Aztec cultures, Nergal's likely influences can be seen through the symbol of the eagle and jaguar, which can be found adorned on many of their sacrificial altars and ritualistic temples. This provides evidence to correlate back to his role as God L within the Maya culture. Besides God L, the beings of Tezcatlipoca and Huitzilopochtli also played a significant part in the corruption of the Aztec people through the practice of blood sacrifice and war, and together, helped to permanently corrupt these ancient civilizations.

It's important to remember that God L, Tezcatlipoca, and Huitzilopochtli only managed to succeed in corrupting these cultures because they were impersonating the serpent-dragon gods. That's the reason why there's still so much confusion surrounding the roles that each of these beings and deities played. This common theme of impersonation and corruption by the Anunnaki can be seen all through history, and only by separating out the facts can we finally discover what the truth really is.

It shouldn't be seen as a coincidence then that this very same tactic was later used by Cortés in conquering the Aztec civilization of Mexico, as he was also impersonating the plumed serpent god of Quetzalcoatl. According to records, Cortés was only able to accomplish this feat because he looked somewhat similar to the feathered serpent god Quetzalcoatl, who the indigenous people of the region considered to be a tall elderly man with a long white beard. I would like to strongly point out that this description of Quetzalcoatl is significant to consider, not only because it correlates with what Viracocha is supposed to have looked like in physical form, but suggests that he originally came from outside the region since these indigenous cultures don't have the ability to grow facial hair. It would, therefore, be illogical to conclude that those who created the grand civilizations of the Maya, Aztec, and Inca civilizations with the knowledge of the cosmos and higher consciousness, would also be involved in their later corruption.

Additional evidence that helps to show that other beings and entities were responsible for the practice of blood sacrifice and war in these cultures can be found in the ruins of the Aztec, Toltec, and Maya civilizations of Mexico. Various steles and murals from the Toltec and Aztec cultures contain depictions of eagles consuming human hearts with blood draining from them. In some cases, the eagles are even shown using their beaks to pierce the human hearts in order to consume their blood. The most important thing to understand in separating the influences of the eagle and serpent gods is that many of these past societies were unaware of the internal struggle going on within these powerful beings and simply thought that "their" god was playing both roles.

This confusion led to many depictions of both the eagle and serpent taking part in blood sacrifice when evidence actually shows that those who influenced Quetzalcoatl-Kukulkan had already left these civilizations long before and moved on to other parts of the world. However, despite this ongoing confusion, some of these indigenous cultures of the Americas still managed to leave behind extensive clues to show the true version of what occurred long ago with these malevolent beings. One of the best examples that still exists today to show this ancient struggle can be found at the famous site of Chichen Itza in the Yucatan Peninsula.

Located in a quiet corner away from the crowds, The Platform of Eagles and Jaguars (also called the House of Eagles), shows multiple depictions that contain both the serpent and dragon symbols of Kukulkan, as well as the later influences of God L, likely played by Nergal. Similar to many of the other edifices found in Mesoamerican cultures of the region, the House of Eagles portrays symbols that include both the jaguar as well as the eagle, who can be seen clutching a human heart that's ready to be consumed.

In some cases, these "hearts" may also be a representation of the symbolic domination over the "seed of knowledge" or pine cone, which was historically shown to represent higher wisdom and the human pineal gland. This depiction can be seen below in Figure 8. Look closely at this image, as it helps to explain the truth behind who influenced these civilizations over different time periods.

Figure 8

The depictions found on The Platform of Eagles and Jaguars are remarkably similar to those seen in the Toltec and Aztec cultures, and provides correlating evidence to link back to the influences of the Mayan deity known as God L. Much of this makes logical sense when you consider that the traits shared by God L closely mimic those of Nergal, a son of Enlil, who took on a deceptive and negative role in the underworld. Furthermore, Nergal was the only deity in the underworld that carried the symbols of the eagle and jaguar. These clues help to piece together the events of history for us to better understand the complexity of our reality. That's why so much confusion still exists surrounding these cultures from antiquity and all the influences they've had in the past.

While spending time researching in the field, I

frequently brought up the significance of these symbols to many of the tour guides and local experts I came across. In most cases, I was given a variety of antiquated and illogical answers to help explain their true meanings. Most of these explanations never even considered the idea of outside intervention, or why these eagle and serpent depictions can be found in ancient cultures across the planet. According to some of these local experts and guides, the common occurrence of these symbols was simply a means of sheer coincidence or just a representation of the various human archetypes. This answer shouldn't be a surprise considering that after the Spanish conquistadors ransacked and destroyed these native cultures of the Americas, they then created their own version of events, based on their biased perspective, to replace the one that existed before. This repetitive theme has occurred throughout history and is one of the main reasons that so much information has become lost.

To me, the fact that the symbols of the eagle and serpent are shared by civilizations across the world is undeniable evidence to show that at one time they all had common influences. Some of these cultures were separated by thousands of miles of rough terrain and vast oceans, and the logical and objective mind must recognize that it's far more than merely a random coincidence. Remember, there are no such things as coincidences, only synchronistic connections. Further evidence that supports these conclusions can be found in the Americas, within many of the statues and ruins left behind by these past cultures.

The Toltec and Aztec civilizations of Mexico called the plumed serpent god "Quetzalcoatl," while the Maya referred to him as "Kukulkan." In South America, this wisdom bringer was known as "Viracocha," who is frequently portrayed holding a staff with two serpents on each end. Viracocha was extensively worshipped throughout South America, which is the reason why many of the indigenous cultures referred to this region as *Ameruca* which meant: "land of the feathered or winged serpents." This information represents a nearly forgotten connection back to the true origins of the name "America," and provides further evidence to show that these serpent-dragon gods of the Inca, Maya, and Aztec all came from a common influence. That's the reason why we see so many similarities with the pyramids of Egypt and those found in Mexico, located over 7,000 miles away.

Viracocha, also called "Ticci Viracocha" or "Tiki," was worshipped as a creator god by the Inca and Tiwanaku cultures and was described as being a tall, elderly-bearded man, just as Quetzalcoatl was. Evidence indicates that Viracocha was likely a high priest from Atlantis, who was closely affiliated with both Quetzalcoatl and Kukulkan during the Pre-Diluvian time period, long before Francisco Pizarro landed on its shores. That's why ancient legends and inscriptions contain details of the great flood since many of these advanced civilizations of the region existed *before* 11,000 years ago. What we commonly think of as the Inca today, are merely distant ancestors of these master stone masons of the past.

Despite the importance of this information, most of society is unaware of the historical connections back to these names, as most have been falsely taught that the origins of America come from the Italian explorer known as Amerigo Vespucci. The logical and objective mind can clearly see the strong correlation that exists for the names "Ameruca" and "America," especially considering who influenced these indigenous cultures long ago.

Just as many of civilizations around the world were separated by the Pre-Diluvian and Postdiluvian time periods, so too were the Inca and Tiwanaku people. That's why ancient structures such as the Gate of the Sun, Sacsayhuamán, or Machu Picchu can be dated to long before the end of the last ice age. As I have previously pointed out, the more recent and less sophisticated stonework that we find on top of these megalithic structures is not representative of who *originally* built them. Most of this recent work that we find was actually done much later, by a far less sophisticated culture. All of this should begin to make sense when you consider the location of where all these ruins were located in relation to the important electromagnet energy ley lines that cross the planet. This relatively new evidence that's beginning to emerge completely rewrites the old doctrine that we've been taught and strongly suggests that our understanding of the past is greatly antiquated.

Another powerful example to show this struggle of the eagle versus the serpent can be found when studying the history of the Spanish Empire, and their conquest of the serpent-dragon civilizations of the Americas. In 1452, the Catholic Church began issuing papal bulls which granted certain privileges and rights to promote missionary work and to secure new lands for the growing Spanish and Portuguese Empires. Between the years of 1492, 1519, and 1532, the Spanish Empire successfully launched three large military campaigns in the Americas (led by Columbus, Cortés, and Pizarro), in order to systematically gain control of new territory, as well as to acquire rare resources for the empire, such as gold and silver.

The Spanish conquest of the Americas claimed the lives of hundreds of thousands of indigenous people and led to the eventual collapse of nearly every culture in the region. From the Puebloan and Hopi of the Southwest United States to the Aztec and Maya of Mexico, and the Inca of South America, these civilizations were systematically wiped out by the Spanish, and their resources and artifacts were stolen. Many of the rare artifacts and sacred texts that were plundered were later taken back to Rome, where they were locked away and sealed in underground vaults, such as beneath the Vatican, to hide their secrets.

Society is taught that these conquistadors of the Americas were heroes and to revere their actions as admirable, yet the facts of history tell a far different story. In the version we're given in school, Christopher Columbus was sent by Spain westward across the Atlantic Ocean, to locate a new trade route to Asia. This deception can be easily exposed when objectively studying the historical account of these events.

When Columbus first reached the Americas in 1492 (near the present-day Bahamas), he was met by the peaceful Lucayan people of the region, a branch of the Taíno tribe that lived throughout the Caribbean islands. Columbus immediately began interrogating them after noticing the gold jewelry they were wearing around their necks. The next action Columbus took (while *supposedly* searching for a western trade route) was to take slaves of the Lucayan people and force them into leading his party to where they had acquired the gold. This information greatly contradicts what we've been taught and provides compelling evidence to show the *true* purpose for his journey to the "New World."

Further evidence to back up this claim comes from studying the specific locations Christopher Columbus visited while in the New World. Over the course of several years, Columbus returned multiple times to Cuba and Hispaniola to acquire its extensive gold deposits. Each time he returned to Spain, Columbus brought back with him a ship full of slaves and large amounts of gold he had plundered from the region. The gold mining in the Caribbean was done almost entirely by the native people, through back-breaking labor and brutal working conditions. In fact, the conditions were often so bad that over the course of several years, most of the indigenous workers died while working in the mines. We may never know just how many people perished in the Caribbean at the hands of these conquistadors, as many of those records were *somehow* lost and left out of most of our history books.

After Columbus and his men had successfully mapped out the Caribbean and acquired the majority its gold, the Spanish Empire then turned their sights to conquering the mainland of Mexico, where they knew that great wealth could be found with the Aztec civilization. In the year 1519, Hernán Cortés and his men landed on the eastern shores of Mexico, near the present-day town of Veracruz, after Cortés deliberately beached most of his ships and forced his men to forge inland with him. Cortés claimed that the reason for this strange action was that the ships were incapable of sailing due to shipworm. The real reason that he did this was that he knew that most of his men were apprehensive about the idea of invading

Mexico, and he feared they would attempt a mutiny and try to return to Cuba.

After establishing the town of Veracruz, Cortés and his men quickly moved inland towards the capital city of Tenochtitlan, with little resistance from the Aztec. Cortés was only able to accomplish this monumental feat after implementing three key strategies. The first was that Cortés managed to trick the Aztec people, including their leader Moctezuma, into believing that he was the returning serpent god of Quetzalcoatl. With his guard down, Moctezuma was captured by Cortés and held for ransom, leading to widespread panic and disorder throughout the Aztec Empire. Cortés and his army then strategically cut off vital food and water supplies to the city of Tenochtitlan and proceeded to massacre the Aztec people by the thousands, leveling most of the city to the ground. On top of the ashes of Tenochtitlan, modern-day Mexico City was then built under the shadow of the watchful eye of the Catholic Church.

After Cortés and his armies had successfully conquered the Aztec, they realized that much of the gold they had seized did not originate from Mexico, but came from elsewhere. Spain later learned of the existence of an extensive trading route that connected from central Mexico, southward, all the way to the Inca civilization of South America. After years of preparation, Spain sent a new "soldier" of the church named Francisco Pizarro to conquer the land of the Inca and plunder its vast gold reserves. But is that really all they were after? Archeological evidence suggests that of all the ancient cultures in the Americas, the great megalithic civilizations of Peru and Bolivia were the most sophisticated of all. However, as I have stated previously, evidence shows that these advanced cultures may pre-date what we think of as the Inca by hundreds if not thousands of years, and the indigenous people Pizarro encountered were mostly made up of their descendants.

In 1531, Francisco Pizarro and a small army landed on the coast of Ecuador, in the present-day province of Coaque, where they were immediately greeted with hostility by the indigenous tribes of the region. After fighting in the bloody conflict known as the Battle of Puná, Pizarro was later joined by Hernando De Soto, along with additional reinforcements, who helped him establish the first Spanish settlement in Peru, known as San Miguel de Piura. With an army of around 200 men, including cavalry, Pizarro moved inland towards the heart of Peru, where he contacted the Inca leader known as Atahualpa. Atahualpa agreed to meet the following day in Cajamarca, where Pizarro attempted to convert him over to Christianity. After repeated attempts, Atahualpa turned down Pizarro's request, angrily stating, "I will be no man's tributary." This decision by Atahualpa led Pizarro and his army to brutally attack the Inca in one of the largest battles of the Americas on November 16th, 1532, known as the Battle of Cajamarca.

During the Battle of Cajamarca, thousands of Inca were slaughtered by Pizarro and his army, most of whom were unarmed consorts of Atahualpa. Following similar tactics as Cortés in Mexico, Pizarro captured the Inca leader Atahualpa and threatened to kill him unless an entire building was filled with gold. After the Inca had fulfilled the ransom request, Pizarro proceeded to execute Atahualpa anyway, which eventually led to the entire collapse of the Inca Empire, years later. This tragedy done to the Inca is sadly echoed by nearly every indigenous culture of the Americas, and acts as a striking reminder to show the destructive influences that these war empires of the eagle have had throughout history. Should these men really be revered as heroes? Perhaps in the future, once society learns the truth about these past events, we can finally honor these fallen civilizations properly, and all that they once represented.

The Flag of Mexico acts as one of the most powerful symbols to show the historic conquering of the serpent-dragon civilizations of the Americas, both on a physical level and non-physical level. It's important to point out that the conquering of the Americas was part of a much larger plan to promote Christianity as the dominant religion of the world. As I discussed previously, many of these old pagan groups were part of what was known as the Old Religion, which was considered a serious threat to the rise of the Christian church. The most targeted of these groups were known as the Druids, who were eventually forced to retreat to the region of Ireland, Wales, and northern Britain. The Druids represented one of the *last* societies on the planet that still practiced the ancient Gnostic and Egyptian teachings from antiquity, as most of the others had already been eradicated and destroyed long ago.

The purpose of this cleansing of the Druids was done to destroy the great legacy of these serpent-dragon teachers from the past, and all the important knowledge they left behind. This "last stand" by the Druids is best shown in the Irish holiday known as Saint Patrick's Day, which I briefly discussed before. I would like to point out that while I will be specifically speaking about Ireland in this example, this cleansing occurred across the entire region. It's important to remember that in *many* cases, the religious term "saint" refers more to loyalty to the church, and less so to their benevolent actions. So, what really is the truth about this holiday?

In the early 17th century, a bishop known as Saint Patrick (whose father was a Roman official), was tasked by the church with the removal of all the "snakes" from Ireland. On the surface this may seem pretty straightforward, however, if one looks into the climate of Ireland and its relative latitude, they quickly find out that there have *never* been any snakes living there. Instead, the term "snakes" is being used as a metaphor for pagans and Druids. Just as the early Gnostics were called evil snakes and demonized by the Christian church, these Druid and pagan groups were also targeted and were either rounded up and forcefully removed or exterminated from the region.

Over the course of several hundred years, a systematic eradication of the Gnostic and Druid people took place from northern Ireland and Britain, southward across Europe and into the Middle East and Africa. This organized "cleansing" led to the deaths of thousands of innocent people and the loss of countless important texts and rare artifacts. Yet at the same time, most of society is completely unaware of the true nature of what this grotesque holiday represents, hidden behind a smokescreen of green leprechauns, alcohol, and false Irish pride. Just as with the story of the Flag of Mexico, the facts and events of history have been cleverly manipulated to hide the truth, while at the same time creating the illusion that these were great heroes. The evidence clearly portrays a far different picture than what we've been told, showing that many of these saints and conquistadors were not really heroes at all, and eventually the history books will reflect that.

When looking at the rise and fall of these conquering eagle empires throughout history, and the destruction of the serpent-dragon societies around the world, the symbolism and traits shared between them is impossible to ignore any longer. We must objectively remember that many of these cultures were scattered across enormous distance, sometimes separated by vast oceans and impossible terrain, and yet somehow, they all "randomly" worshipped the same gods and shared the same symbols? To me, it's clear that both the Anunnaki gods and ancient Atlanteans played a major role in influencing these civilizations of the past.

At some point, our society will have to decide if it's ready to take charge of its own future, instead of allowing others to dictate it for us. I'm confident that once this hidden struggle of the eagle and serpent is finally realized, everything in our reality will change. Until that time comes, each one of us must decide which path we will ultimately take in life; one that's guided either by the light of higher knowledge and wisdom, or the darkness of ignorance, materialism, and war. Which path will you take?

Continue on with me to the next chapter where we seek to unravel the mysteries of Earth and the Solar System, as well as the intelligent design behind the universe, and our role in this great "Stage of Time." (1,2,3,8,9,10,11,13,14,15,16,17,18,19,20,21)

CHAPTER 4

EARTH, THE UNIVERSE, AND STAGE OF TIME

What is our true purpose here? According to ancient texts, each soul on Earth is here to learn valuable lessons in order to grow on a spiritual and conscious level. That's why each soul on the planet is experiencing their own unique perspective for how they view and decipher the reality that surrounds them. This individual perspective is derived from a multitude of complex factors, all of which begin at a very young age. Those factors lead to either raising a person's awareness or limiting its potential through the means of negative stimuli or a lack of motivation. Together, all of these shared experiences combine to create the story of humanity, or what I commonly refer to as "our story."

On a deeper level, this story represents the ongoing narrative for the entire human race, which is based on the particular path we've collectively decided to take as a species. This delicate timeline is the key to our future, as our individual contributions here echo across all of time. Even on a minor scale, the smallest of our actions can ripple outward and have a long-lasting effect on far more than most realize. This principle is what's known as the butterfly effect in chaos theory. Sadly, despite the sheer importance of this concept to the framework and outcome of our reality, most people have been conditioned over time to largely ignore their actions, as well as how they could affect others around them. This mentality is especially true regarding the treatment of planet Earth and the long-term outcome of humanity as a whole.

William Shakespeare once famously wrote, "All the world's a stage, and all the men and women merely players; they have their exits and their entrances; and one man in his time plays many parts." Ponder on those words and think deeply about what they could mean on a higher level for both our existence here on Earth, as well as the specific role that we each decide to play in society. The sheer ingenuity and power behind this quote is one of the main influences for why I chose the title: *The Stage of Time*. Based on that mindset, I feel that it's critical that society finally understands that collectively, we're experiencing nearly all aspects of duality at the same time, and then unknowingly manifesting those experiences into our physical reality. The real question is, which side of duality will we collectively choose to follow?

Continuing along with this analogy of a grand "stage," each person on the planet *must* make the important choice of which role they'll decide to take on in this life. Whether that means becoming a hero, a villain, or playing the part of an extra, all of us have the ability to choose the specific path we want to follow. If someone is unaware of their individual role within this grand stage of mental and physical expression, then they're likely what I call an extra. It's important to understand that without these "extras" there would simply be no reason for the collective story of humanity to exist in the first place. Furthermore, any individual who considers themselves an extra can become a hero or a villain at any time based on the law of free will and the power of *choice*. Those who consider themselves an extra, hero, or villain, are all simply actors playing a different role in reality. This distinction of purpose reflects the specific decisions that each of us will decide to make in life, which will ultimately determine how we'll be remembered in the future.

The great challenge and struggle of free will became which role or persona each of us would decide to take on based on the influences we received. On a larger scale, the impact of those decisions can ripple out and affect far more than we realize. This is the primary reason why there has been so much interest by the Anunnaki and other entities over the outcome of mankind. To fully explain how this "Stage of Time" really works, we'll need to review the fundamentals of superstring theory, vibration, and the different dimensions. But before we dive any deeper into particle physics and the nature of reality, we must first develop a better understanding of the Solar System and our vast galactic neighborhood.

According to geologic and archeological records, between 10,000 and 12,800 years ago a series of violent cataclysms took place on the Earth that caused a sudden end to the last ice age, massive global floods, and a large extinction of land animals across the Northern

Hemisphere. This disaster led to the destruction of most of the advanced civilizations around the world, causing a reset button on humanity and turning their legacy into nothing more than a myth by most of society. This was known as the Antediluvian or Pre-Diluvian time period, which I discussed in detail in previous chapters. So, what exactly caused these devastating events to take place, and will they happen again? To help answer those questions we need to review a brief history of the Solar System, the Sun, and the mysteries that surround the Kuiper Belt.

Ice core data from Greenland supports the theory that the Earth experiences continuous cycles of destruction and climate change as part of a natural process, which is one of the *main* reasons why so many advanced megalithic civilizations of the past, such as the Atlanteans, Pre-Inca, Mesopotamians, Pre-Dynastic Egyptians, and Indus Valley Civilizations were wiped out and became nearly lost to time. To make things even more complicated, some of the less developed indigenous cultures that managed to survive these disasters moved into these ancient sites afterward and attempted to imitate their sophisticated building techniques, without success.

That's why in places such as Peru and Mexico, we find younger construction that was done on top of the older megalithic structures at the bottom. To me, this evidence strongly suggests that the knowledge and influences imparted by the Anunnaki became less and less over time. The most important questions that remain are, what could have caused these cataclysms, and where did the Anunnaki come from?

Planet Nine and Secrets of the Solar System

The first place we need to start is by defining and separating two terms that have been frequently used in conjunction with one another but are in fact not related. Those two terms are Nibiru and Planet X. It's important that I point out that Planet X is now referred to as Planet Nine, based on the demotion of Pluto. Therefore, for the purposes of accuracy, I will be referring to this object in the outer Solar System as Planet Nine, but technically they're the same thing. Remember, the most effective means of separating out what the truth is from the many lies and deceptions that have been taught to us is by always following the scientific evidence, and then combining objective logic and intuition to formulate plausible conclusions.

To better define and separate the terms Nibiru and Planet Nine, we must review a few key areas first, including what the ancient Sumerians knew about the Solar System, the tablets of the Enuma Elish, and the astronomical evidence proving the existence of Planet Nine. I would like to strongly point out that the information I'm about to present is *not* derived by simply regurgitating any one researcher's viewpoints, but is based solely on objectively studying the evidence that exists. The challenge today has become how to separate out all the misinformation that constantly bombards us from what the truth really is. This has never been truer regarding Nibiru and Planet Nine (previously called Planet X).

The ancient Sumerians claimed that their knowledge of the stars, writing, agriculture, mathematics, and governing structures were all lowered from *heaven* by great gods they called the Anunnaki. Unfortunately, the term heaven still carries a heavy stigma throughout most of society due to its frequent use in many of the world's religions, which often cloud its real meaning. It should be apparent by now that these beings who are referred to as the "Anunnaki" are not originally from this planet since the word "ki" references the name of Earth, with their full name translating to mean: "Those who Anu sent from heaven **to** Earth." This indicates that they were *sent* here. From where though? We'll be reviewing that area in more detail later. So, what really did the Sumerians know about the Anunnaki and the Solar System?

The ancient cylinder seal from Mesopotamia known as VA-243 represents a scale model of the entire Solar System, which includes our central Sun and the planets that revolve around it. Beyond the small details and confusion that still surrounds exactly what VA-243 is portraying, the main point I want to make about this cylinder seal is that it shows that the Sumerian people knew precise details about the planets of the Solar System long before the first telescopes were ever invented. This is important because it suggests that these ancient civilizations were far more advanced than what we've been told, as they understood details about our cosmic neighborhood that we're just now "discovering" today. The two questions that remain are: How exactly could the Sumerians have known so much about the Solar System, and does VA-243 really show evidence of Planet Nine?

When comparing the size ratios depicted in VA-243 to the known ratios and dimensions of the planets in the Solar System, strong correlations can be made for each of the planets, including Pluto. This leaves only one, whose identity remains controversial. Many argue that VA-243 provides proof of the existence of a new planet, while others say it's the destroyed remnants of one from long ago. Regardless of what the exact truth is behind VA-243, it should still be regarded as one of the most important cylinder seals ever recovered, since it suggests that the Sumerians, and other early cultures, knew a vast amount about the Solar System long before the first telescopes were invented. These anomalies simply can't be ignored any longer and strongly support the hypothesis that the Sumerians were *given* this knowledge by beings they called the Anunnaki.

One of the ongoing challenges with correctly deciphering cuneiform tablets is determining exactly what they meant by certain terms, such as Nibiru. In Hebrew, the name Nibiru translates to "the crossing," which is interesting since we find numerous murals and statues from Mesopotamia that depict the Anunnaki wearing the early figure of the cross around their necks. This is, of course, *thousands* of years before modern religions adopted it. The cross, and its many variations such as the Egyptian ankh, were important to different cultures around the world and represented the "crossing" of mind, body, and soul to reach Kundalini and eternal life. Eventually, the true meaning behind this sacred symbol became corrupted and nearly lost over time, just as with the swastika. So then, what is Nibiru actually referencing? Let's go deeper.

Some researchers argue that Nibiru represents planet Jupiter and has been a mistranslation by Zechariah Sitchin. At the same time, Sitchin claims that Nibiru is a rogue planet that crosses through the Solar System every

3,600 years. So, what exactly is the truth? One of the most difficult aspects of deciphering these ancient texts and then incorporating them into historical facts, is that they are often written as parables which contain extensive symbolism and metaphors. This style of writing has led to great confusion among most mainstream experts and academics over precisely what they meant.

The conclusions I'm about to present suggests that much of what we've been told about Nibiru may be incorrect. However, that doesn't mean that another planet doesn't exist in the Solar System. In fact, the data gathered by Robert Harrington, Thomas Van Flandern, and Rodney Gomez strongly points to the existence of an unknown planet that's located in the far outer rim of the Solar System. This "unknown" planet, collectively known as Planet Nine, has a relative orbit and position that greatly differs from the findings presented by Sitchin but is still real nonetheless. Now, let's review the evidence that backs up that statement.

After careful consideration, I've determined that Zechariah Sitchin may have mistranslated the cuneiform tablets that mention the term Nibiru, and then created a false hypothesis regarding its orbit. This was largely due to the confusion that still surrounds the number 3,600. My analysis has revealed that the term Nibiru is likely referencing either one of two things. It either represents the symbolic crossing of energy between the mind, body, and soul to reach Kundalini or the planet Jupiter. What's interesting about the planet Jupiter is that it's known as the great "balancer" of the Solar System and is the *only* planet whose center mass (known as the barycenter), lies outside the volume of the sun. What that means is that the mass of Jupiter is so large that its orbit is collectively shared through a combined center of gravity with the sun. However, if I had to choose one definition based on the evidence, I would say the term Nibiru represents the crossing of energy to reach Kundalini.

Despite this minor hiccup in translation by Sitchin, there remains extensive evidence which suggests that Planet Nine exists somewhere in the outer Solar System, but with an orbital position which is likely to be found somewhere near the edge of the Kuiper Belt. This minor mistake by Zechariah Sitchin does not mean he created the entire story of the Anunnaki, or that he mistranslated most of these ancient texts. What it means is that he simply made an error about the term Nibiru and the true meaning of the number 3,600. In retrospect, most of Sitchin's base translations are quite accurate and should still be considered an important source for reference. It's important that I mention that I still hold great respect and admiration for the work done by him. Remember, *all* of us make mistakes at times, that's why the individual must always remain objective with incoming information. Now having said that, what is the evidence that supports these conclusions?

The Inuit people of Northern Canada have hunted for and gathered food using the position of the stars for navigation for hundreds of years, and have woven this connected relationship into the very fabric of their society. Over the last ten years, many of the Inuit community elders have reached out in alarm to warn others that the alignments of the star constellations, sun, and moon have shifted, and are no longer in the same position as before. As it turns out, the Inuit were right. Scientists have become increasingly alarmed at the rapid changes they've observed with the wobbling of the Earth's axis and a shifting of the magnetic north pole. So, what exactly could be causing these changes to the Earth and could they be related to the Sun or possibly even the distant influences of Planet Nine? Let's dig into the evidence to find answers.

The hunt for Planet Nine began in 1846, following new discoveries that showed that Neptune's orbit was being disrupted by an unknown object. Some astronomers postulated that these anomalies may be the result of an unidentified planet, whose gravitational force was affecting the outer planets of the Solar System. With the discovery of Pluto in 1930, it was initially thought that this celestial body was responsible for Neptune's observed gravitational disruptions. However, following the detection of a moon orbiting the planet in 1978 named Charon, the mass of Pluto was then able to be determined, showing that it was insufficient to account for Neptune's unusual orbit. This meant that an unidentified planet *must* exist in the far outer reaches of the Solar System, with a mass more than *four* times that of Earth.

Between the years of 1972 and 1973, NASA launched two space probes to explore and study the outer reaches of the Solar System. Besides exploration, the primary goal of these two probes, known as Pioneer 10 and 11, was to help explain the strange anomalies seen to the orbits of Uranus and Neptune. Astronomical observation of these two planets showed that some outside force was tilting and pulling at their orbits from a great distance away. To identify these anomalies, NASA equipped the Pioneer probes with infrared sensors to detect any heat signatures that could be found from any unknown planetary bodies that could exist out there.

In 1983, the newly launched IRAS satellite began sending back images which showed what looked like a large mysterious planetary body engulfed in a winged disk of gas, following a highly unusual ecliptic orbit. Could this have been the first image ever captured of Planet Nine? In 1992, NASA released a shocking press statement which stated:

"Unexplained deviations in the orbits of Uranus and Neptune point to a large outer Solar System body of 4 to 8 Earth masses on a highly tilted orbit, beyond 7 billion miles from the Sun."

Experts postulated that this new planetary body helped to explain the strange orbit observed for Pluto, which is considered far outside the rest of the planets' orbits within the inner Solar System. They determined that Pluto was likely once a moon of Neptune or Saturn, which was later thrust into its current orbit by the influences of this unknown planetary body.

In 1987, The _New Illustrated Science and Invention Encyclopedia, Vol. 18_ was released which contained detailed astronomical data that not only described the existence of Planet Nine, but a previously unknown dwarf star that it revolves around. It's important to understand that this astronomical evidence is _solely_ based on the findings from these two Pioneer Probes and isn't based on someone's biased opinion. So then, why haven't more people heard about this discovery? That's the underlying reason this data was later covered up by NASA, along with many other important facts about the

Solar System. That's why these scientific findings are so important to review and understand since they help to explain so much about the outer Solar System.

As hard as it may be to accept, we must remember that what the mainstream frequently touts as nothing more than bogus "conspiracies theories" are often very real. The educational doctrine that's taught to society is not always based on the unbiased facts. This conclusion isn't simply derived from empty conspiracy paranoia, but from logical reasoning and objectively studying the unbiased facts. This evidence is a perfect example of just how controlled information has become, especially from NASA. Regarding the 1987 encyclopedia, I find it peculiar that only the picture was kept, and very little was mentioned regarding the astonishing discoveries made by Pioneer 10. That most likely means that what Pioneer 10 discovered was redacted *before* it was published.

On page 2,488 of the _New Illustrated Science and Invention Encyclopedia, Vol. 18_ it says:

"Pioneer 10 became the first craft to pass into interstellar space in 1983. The diagram shows the path of the two Pioneer probes."

Even though Pioneer 11 may have been unsuccessful at detecting any new planetary objects, Pioneer 10 more than made up for it. What Pioneer 10 detected that was so important was the discovery of two previously unknown objects located well beyond the Kuiper Belt. The first is listed as a dead star, located more than 50 billion miles from Earth. The second is referred to as the tenth planet and found almost 5 billion miles away. This new planet (initially nicknamed Planet X and later Planet Nine) helps to provide strong evidence to explain why comets and planets found in the outer Solar System exhibit perturbations in their orbits. In 1992, astronomers made an important discovery in the region of Pluto when they discovered an enormous asteroid and comet field they called the Kuiper Belt. This asteroid and comet field was determined to be 100 to 200 times larger than the one found between Mars and Jupiter, containing over 100,000 previously unknown comets and asteroids. This new discovery led to an extensive study of the Kuiper Belt and Taurid meteor stream to determine how they could affect the Earth in the future. The real question is, what role did they play in Earth's past?

Thomas Van Flandern was an American astronomer and scientist who became increasingly frustrated with the mainstream view that was being taught to society regarding the facts of history, astronomy, and even the nature of reality itself. In the early 1980's he gave a profound quote which stated:

"Events in my life caused me to start questioning my goals and the correctness of everything I had learned. In matters of religion, medicine, biology, physics, and other fields, I came to discover that reality differed seriously from what I had been taught."

I find this quote from Thomas Van Flandern to be both brilliant and extremely accurate, correlating strikingly well with many of my own conclusions. What also makes this quote especially impressive is the fact that it was said nearly 40 years ago. Before making this bold statement,

Thomas had developed a keen interest in the gravitational protrusions seen with the orbits of Neptune and Uranus, and he studied every piece of astronomical data he could get his hands on to determine what could be causing the anomalies. After reviewing the findings gathered from Pioneer 10, he contacted his friend Robert Harrington to seek further answers.

Robert Harrington was the head astronomer at the United States Naval Observatory and like Flandern, he became enamored by what could be causing the abnormal orbits of Neptune and Uranus. After comparing notes with Flandern, Harrington pushed forward, determined to find out the truth despite the increasing pressure he was facing on a daily basis. Harrington realized that Planet Nine was the most likely candidate to explain these anomalies and using the data gathered from Pioneer 10, determined that this mysterious, rogue planet was likely found in the region of Scorpius.

In 1993, after extensively reviewing the findings gathered from the IRAS satellite and Pioneer 10, Harrington traveled to the southern tip of New Zealand where it's believed he observed Planet Nine on an 8-inch telescope. After this discovery was made, Robert Harrington was diagnosed with throat cancer and died, where his work was immediately debunked by NASA as nothing more than mathematical errors. This brought a temporary halt to the search for Planet Nine until years later when in 2012, an important discovery was made by astronomer Rodney Gomes.

Rodney Gomes is an astronomer from the National Observatory of Brazil, and in 2012, he determined that some unknown object was affecting the orbital paths of many of the asteroids and comets found within the

Kuiper Belt region. He postulated that a new, unknown planetary body *must* be responsible for these orbital anomalies. These conclusions by Rodney Gomes correlate strikingly well with those previously given by Flandern and Harrington, and greatly helps to explain the unusual orbits of Neptune and Uranus, as well as the abrupt boundary that exists for the Kuiper Belt. These important findings were so cleverly covered up and suppressed that most aren't even aware they exist at all.

Robert Harrington and Thomas Van Flandern proposed that Planet Nine has an elliptical orbit of roughly 10,000-20,000 years, and depending on the pass, either crosses or closely approaches the edge of the Kuiper Belt. These calculations provide evidence to show that Planet Nine doesn't penetrate as deep into the inner Solar System as some have stated. Instead, the most pronounced effects to Earth are likely from a combination of dislodged comets, asteroids, and gravitational disruptions.

Let's consider for a moment that if Planet Nine has an elliptical orbit of between 10,000-20,000 years (as postulated by Harrington and Flandern), then it could potentially mean that each time the planet passes near or through the Kuiper Belt, large asteroids and comets could be hurdled towards the Earth. These disruptions to the Kuiper Belt, in conjunction with destructive solar outbursts and pole shifts, are likely the main catalysts behind why so many ancient civilizations in the past disappeared.

It's interesting to learn that the Egyptian text known as the Kolbrin Bible refers to a rogue object found in our outer Solar System as "the destroyer." Instead of perceiving human history in a simplistic and linear way, we should view it as cyclical in nature. The reason so much of this information has been suppressed and hidden for so long is that it would dramatically alter our understanding of astronomy and the early history of the Solar System.

This decision made by NASA to hide the existence of Planet Nine was not due to a lack of information or conclusive evidence, but rather, to protect the public from panic and to control the educational doctrine taught to society. How do you think people would react if they found out that a rogue planet in the outer Solar System periodically disturbs comets and asteroids that could hit Earth and cause mass extinctions?

One of the best examples to show the influences from Planet Nine can be seen with the unusual orbital path taken by Halley's Comet. That's why it's fascinating to learn that the Anglo-Saxons of Great Britain extensively studied the path of Halley's comet and may have even revealed clues to Planet Nine in some of their writings and murals. Even though there is compelling evidence to show that Planet Nine is real, most are unwilling to do their own research and objectively review the scientific data for themselves. Remember, in order to become a successful researcher of the truth, it's important to always remain open-minded to new information and only allow evidence and logic to dictate your conclusions.

The untimely deaths of Robert Harrington and Thomas Van Flandern meant that neither of them would be able to defend their astronomical findings in the future regarding Planet Nine. This could potentially lead to their important accomplishments becoming nothing more than a footnote in the history books. I for one *refuse* to allow this atrocity to happen. The data gathered by the Pioneer

10 probe, along with the theories proposed by Harrington, Flandern, and Gomes about Planet Nine and the Kuiper Belt helps to finally explain the anomalies observed in the outer Solar System, as well as why there have been continuous cycles of destruction throughout Earth's history. This leads us to two important questions that remain unanswered, what are the origins of life on Earth, and what is the truth behind evolution?

Evolution and Sentient Life in the Universe

Fossil records indicate that around 3.5 billion years ago the Earth cooled enough to support the first lifeforms on its surface. Over time, as the environment became optimal, more complex lifeforms began to appear, first as single-celled prokaryotic organisms, and later as multicellular eukaryotes. But the real question is, where did they come from? According to my research, this "seeding" of life likely came from a combination of both panspermia and intelligent outside influences. As hard as that may be for some to accept, ancient cultures across the world have frequently mentioned that "sky gods" originally seeded life on the planet and even assisted some of them during times of great disaster.

Consider for a moment the vast amount of life that's still present on the Earth, even today. How could Darwinian evolution account for the millions of unique species we find in nearly every environment on the planet? Especially considering that these species would have had to survive through countless cycles of destruction and planet-wide extinctions. To me, this is further evidence to show that outside influences *had* to be involved in its early seeding and continued maintenance, or most of these lifeforms would have been wiped out long ago. Using this logic, it seems plausible that the process of complex life appearing and thriving on any given planet is more dependent on the specific "timing" of *when* its environment becomes optimal, and not merely the result of random macroevolutionary traits.

What that means is that as a planet's climate becomes more favorable and less hostile, it could become a candidate for more advanced lifeforms to be seeded there. In fact, any physical changes that are observed with a species over time, based on its unique environment, is what's known as microevolution and not macroevolution. Essentially, the only changes that can occur with a species happen on a very *small* level and not on a major one. That's why I feel that in the future we'll likely need to throw out the incorrect and antiquated model of evolution we've been taught and instead consider new theories for how complex life begins and changes over time.

Today, over eight *million* unique species have been recorded on the Earth, with new discoveries being made every day. If we consider for a moment the Darwinian model of evolution that has been adopted for hundreds of years by modern science, then how could it be possible that all these species originated from nothing more than primordial pools of sludge? Since geologic records indicate that mass extinctions have occurred on a cyclical basis throughout the planet's history, it would have meant that nearly all of life would have been wiped out multiple times. That's why I feel that the old doctrine we've been taught in school regarding the evolution of Homo sapiens is completely illogical if you account for the sheer complexity and unusual anomalies we see within our DNA, physical appearance, and chakra centers that would have been impossible without some kind of outside intervention. To me, these unique traits strongly suggest that human beings are the product of past DNA manipulation from a supreme race.

Consider for a moment that if humans are derived from nothing more than an evolved ape, as proposed by the theories of Darwinism-with no outside intervention, then why don't we *still* see apes changing on an evolutionary level today? Yet throughout human history, no one has *ever* documented the existence of any apes that have been observed changing on a physical level through macroevolution. This strongly supports the hypothesis that evolution happens on a micro and not a macro level, and that larger changes are likely due to a combination of outside influences and panspermia, and not from natural processes.

The brilliant geneticist and researcher Lloyd Pye recognized many of these problems and inaccuracies that exist surrounding Darwin's theories about evolution. Pye extensively studied both the human genome, as well as ancient cuneiform tablets from Mesopotamia, and decided to dedicate much of his life to uncovering the truth about evolution and our past. His work became vital in understanding the link that exists between the abnormal genetic traits found within the human genome, known as non-coding DNA or "junk" DNA, with the large brain size common to Homo sapiens. What Pye uncovered strongly suggests that this non-coding DNA represents the *direct* connection back to the outside influences from advanced beings who tampered with the genome of early hominids over 200,000 years ago.

The reason the term "non-coding" or "junk" was used by many scientists was that this DNA doesn't match *any* other species found on the Earth, and they were unsure of how to categorize it. Some have even gone as far to suggest that the term "junk" was deliberately used to hide its importance, since it may represent the lost connection back to what really separates Homo sapiens from the rest of the animal kingdom. That's why the human genome contains only 46 chromosomes, instead of 48 like most other primates. This fusing together of our chromosomes would have been *impossible* in nature and provides strong evidence to show that humans have been genetically tampered with in the past.

This non-coding DNA is one of the most important aspects of what makes us human beings, even though it represents only a portion of our overall genome. Remember, in terms of understanding DNA, often the smallest percentage differences lead to the most significant physical and mental differences. By connecting these new breakthroughs in human genome sequencing, along with incorporating the information contained within the Atrahasis and Enuma Elish, we can begin to shed light on what's known as the "evolutionary missing link" for human origins. When all this information is connected it begins to make sense as to why certain beings would have wanted to play the role of gods here, either helping to raise human consciousness or in some cases suppress it.

Expanding beyond the Allegory of the Cave metaphor which I extensively discussed in my previous book, *The Illusion of Us*, there's another term that I frequently use in conjunction to help describe the truth behind the structure of our reality I call: "Darwin's Cave." The reason I specifically call it this is that the antiquated theories proposed by Charles Darwin became one of the most significant roadblocks hindering our understanding of early human origins, life in the universe, and our purpose here.

To me, the evidence overwhelmingly supports a far more connected and intelligent universe than the mundane and close-minded viewpoints proposed by Darwin, which confidently states that throughout the trillions of other planets, moons, and star systems, nearly all of them are void of life, and exist as nothing more than lifeless rocks of dust. The far more logical conclusion to make, especially when considering the numerous global extinctions that have occurred in Earth's history, and the theories proposed by Frank Drake, is that life is likely found nearly everywhere, and is far more complex than most realize. Let's expand on these principles further.

Astronomical data shows that the Solar System is located on one of the outer spiral bands of the Milky Way Galaxy. Our closest neighbor, known as the Andromeda Galaxy, is located 2.5 million light years from Earth. To put that into perspective, if we had the ability to travel at the speed of light it would take roughly 2.5 million years to reach it. That time needed, combined with the distance of the location in space, is what's known as "space-time." These astronomically long distances are often used as proof by certain linear-minded individuals to claim that travel between distant planets and star systems would be impossible for any extraterrestrial beings.

On the surface, it would seem they're largely right until you begin to study the properties of wormholes and artificially created stargates. These portals or stargates may represent ancient connections that once existed between distant locations in our galaxy. Could that be the purpose behind the Gate of the Sun in Tiwanaku, South America? Without these shortcuts through space, travel between these locations would be very difficult to achieve. To me, this is the most logical means for how any advanced beings from outside the Solar System could have come to Earth.

According to the Drake equation, scattered throughout the billions of distant planets, solar systems, and galaxies likely exists countless other civilizations, some far more advanced than our own. Meanwhile, at the same time, most of our society is unaware that any life exists beyond our planet, which is cleverly hidden behind a veil of ultimate secrecy and layers of our own ignorance. This false conditioning has helped to create the illusion that we exist in today, where we're taught that our ultimate purpose here is to simply fight over dwindling resources, accumulate wealth, and waste our time and energy on frivolous activities.

The theory of quantum mechanics states that everything in the universe can be defined by its vibratory structure and frequency. From the state of matter to the relative temperature and color of light, these properties can be understood through the lens of what their unique vibratory frequency is. At the same time, string theory states all matter can be categorized and reduced to various strings of energy vibrating at different rates. This is how reality *can* be defined on a purely holographic level to us, allowing all possible expressions and archetypes to exist at nearly the same time. However, that doesn't imply in any way that space is fake.

From the darkest corners of evil, to the most beautiful

moments of love, everything in the universe follows a particular vibratory structure to it. The expression and energy associated with love can *only* exist within a higher vibration, while at the same time, the energy associated with hate and evil is always reflected through a slower vibration. If an individual learns and understands these properties correctly, they will be able to achieve a higher state of energy and conscious awareness. This implies a connection exists between certain colors in the visible light spectrum, such as red and blue, that represent the energetic potential within a sentient being to reach either a higher or lower state. Allow me to explain.

Looking back through history at the colors associated with secret societies, flags, and even political parties, the repetitive use of red and blue can't be ignored. In many ways, the colors of red and blue can be closely associated with the Gnostic understanding of the properties of darkness and light within the human archetypes. Because of the difference in how a human being functions based on their level of vibrational frequency, the colors of red and blue represent either a lower state of energy, shown through the red root chakra, or a higher state of energy, shown through the blue chakra.

It's by no means a coincidence that the human chakra centers just so happen to perfectly match these colors of the visible light spectrum since the energy associated with creativity, wisdom, and self-awareness is represented through our higher chakras. Therefore, if a sentient being is kept in a state that's dominated by their red root chakra through the means of fear, war, and preying on their basic urges, then they will almost *always* remain in their lowest state of consciousness. That's the reason why Thoth refers to us as "the children of men" in the Emerald Tablets.

Consider the idea that advanced beings *could* have the capability of viewing and deciphering the different timelines that exist. Since human behavior can be somewhat predictable at times, a relatively accurate timeline could be plotted by understanding the various cycles of consciousness that occur due to solar changes, as well as the specific location that the Earth is located relative to the galactic center of the Milky Way. For instance, if a particular timeline for Earth features a large catastrophe or devastating nuclear war, sometimes certain events *can* be set into motion to prevent them from ever happening. On a much larger scale, oppression from continuous wars or extended periods of peace can also dramatically alter the potential future of a civilization. The term "as above so below" means that what happens in the higher dimensions and lower dimensions could become manifested into the physical third dimension of our reality. That's why the third dimension represents the ultimate "stage" in the universe.

Throughout the vastness of space, from every distant star shimmering in the night sky, to the farthest known galaxy, there exists a cosmic hierarchy for all of life. The purpose of this hierarchy system is to maintain sovereignty and balance for the uninterrupted development of any sentient beings. The more advanced that a civilization becomes, the more inherent the need is for them to reach higher states of consciousness before self-annihilation or cataclysms occur. According to the Hopi, Maya, and Aztec, this has led to at *least* three different ages of mankind which were all separated by terrible catastrophes, forcing civilizations to start over again.

Somewhat hypothetically speaking, what would the outcome be if an advanced group of beings or entities diverged from this higher perspective, and instead decided to manipulate another sentient lifeform for their own personal benefit? What would human societies have looked like without the influences of the Anunnaki in the past? After all, they're the ones who polluted our timeline by introducing extreme duality and war here. These are the types of questions we must ask in order to see the multitude of possibilities behind what our future could have been.

To better understand the means for how the realm of Earth became ruled by certain beings, and the various influences that the movement of the cosmos plays on the evolution of human consciousness, we must read through the ancient teachings left behind from Thoth to find answers. According to the Quetzalcoatl prophecy, along with the Mayan Calendar, there exist cycles of energy which are governed by "lords" or "cycle masters," who determine the timing of when certain leaps in consciousness will occur. This information also corresponds with what other texts say written by Thoth, such as the Emerald Tablets, which extensively discusses his interaction with these cycle masters on several occasions. That interaction can be read in Emerald Tablet number 7.

Tablet 7 of the Emerald Tablets states:

"Learned I of the Masters of Cycles, wisdom brought from the cycles above. Manifest they in this cycle as guides of man to the knowledge of all."

Thoth goes on to explain that these cycles are ruled by seven lords who govern the various energetic states that exist and then manifests them into mankind through certain timed human incarnations and progressive leaps in consciousness. I would like to point out that to me, it's clear that it's in no way a coincidence that there are seven cycle masters and seven colors in the visible light spectrum. This balance of reality and the significance of the third dimension, is what creates the framework for *The Stage of Time*, and the duality we see between the eagle and serpent. Figure 9 below shows the serpent god Kukulkan in Chichen Itza, Mexico.

Figure 9

It's important that I point out that there are likely *other* entities and beings, besides the Anunnaki, who are involved in this struggle on Earth, some of whom who are quite negative and don't wish for the ascension of human consciousness. Thoth may have referred to them in the Emerald Tablets when he says they're brought forth into this reality using dark magic and blood sacrifice. This practice of black magic and blood sacrifice is considered one of the major reasons for the eventual downfall of Atlantis and represents a warning sign to all of humanity in the future.

Tablet 8 of the Emerald Tablets states:

"Far in the past before Atlantis existed,
men there were who delved into darkness,
using dark magic, calling up beings
from the great deep below us.
Forth came they into this cycle.
Formless were they of another vibration,
existing unseen by the children of earth-men.
Only through blood could they have formed being.
Only through man could they live in the world.

In ages past were they conquered by Masters,
driven below to the place whence they came.
But some there were who remained,
hidden in spaces and planes unknown to man.
Lived they in Atlantis as shadows,
but at times they appeared among men."

Looking back throughout history, a strong connection can be made linking the symbol of the eagle with both war and blood sacrifice. I've discussed this concept in much greater detail in previous chapters, specifically revolving around the Maya and Aztec cultures. This dark path is likely due to the influences of certain entities and beings over time, who sometimes play a deceptive and malevolent role within our reality. Anytime that a religion is based on the consumption of the "blood" of another, it can often be traced back to this.

It should be no surprise then that locations such as Bohemian Grove in California practice mock blood sacrifices, in which presidents and leaders from all over the world regularly attend. Even the famous Manhattan Project can be traced back to its development at Bohemian Grove by Julius Robert Oppenheimer in 1942. This dark truth can be very difficult to accept, but necessary to understand. The more one looks all around us, the more they'll see that war and blood sacrifice, in one form or another, rules much of our world. The Quetzalcoatl prophecy states that there exist certain realms in which "cycle masters" control both energy and human consciousness through.

Tablet 9 of the Emerald Tablets explains these various cycles and dimensions, stating:

"Nine are the interlocked dimensions, and Nine are the cycles of space. Nine are the diffusions of consciousness, and Nine are the worlds within worlds. Nine are the Lords of the cycles that come from above and below."

Mesopotamian cuneiform tablets indicate that the nine dimensions of our reality are controlled and ruled over by the Anunnaki who each maintain unique roles within our reality. The abzu, or Duat, is largely governed by the beings of Enki and Nergal, who together play the roles of both a positive and negative influence in the underworld in order to maintain balance. These roles of duality are mirrored in the higher dimensions as well, which forms the basis for the phrase, "as above so below." That's the reason why the tunnels and shafts found underneath the Sphinx and pyramids of Giza still remain such a mystery since they represent the literal gateways to the underworld. In fact, Thoth states in the Emerald Tablets that these underground tunnels are the location where the famous Hall of Records were kept.

As I discussed previously, the Earth is likely only one of an overwhelming number of habitable planets in our Milky Way Galaxy that contain sentient life, let alone the *billions* of other galaxies we're just now discovering today using the Hubble Telescope. Even if an individual decides to ignore all the evidence pointing towards outside intervention, it's still illogical to conclude that we're all alone. Especially when taking into account the theories of the Drake equation, and the sheer abundance of carbon-based molecules found throughout the universe.

Using this specific logic, along with the evidence found in cylinder seals and ancient texts, it seems highly probable that there are beings and entities who continuously monitor and watch over humanities progress. The Igigi perhaps? Based on the sheer abundance of lifeforms and genetic diversity found on Earth, it may be considered a type of DNA library for some of them. This hypothesis leads to the larger question of whether or not all the species on the planet originated from there, such as humans. To me, this theory is much more plausible than those proposed by Darwin, especially considering the global mass extinctions that have regularly occurred throughout Earth's history, which would have made macroevolution nearly impossible here, at least on a large scale.

This "living library of Earth" as it has been called by some, most likely originated through the means of both panspermia, as well as the outside influences from advanced beings who came here in the past. According to the Enuma Elish, the Anunnaki were responsible for disrupting this delicate harmony and balance with Mother Earth when they arrived here hundreds of thousands of years ago, attempting to play the role of God by tampering with species, the energy of the planet, and bringing with them war and extreme duality. This is where the term "fallen angels" originates from since these beings were severely punished for their actions here.

The Anunna, as they call themselves, then proceeded to take control of the energy and soul reincarnation cycles on the planet, allowing them to decide which human beings could ascend, while the rest remained trapped in an endless loop as low vibrational-energetic slaves. How could that be possible? One clue to help explain this comes from studying the specific ratio of our moon to the Earth, which is considered *highly* unusual compared to other planets we know of. In fact, tests that were done to determine its composition have found that the moon may be completely *hollow* inside. That means that the moon could be partially artificial and being used as a construct to lower the vibrational frequency of the Earth. This explains how the natural harmony of the planet could have been disrupted long ago, as well as why human consciousness has been trapped in such a low vibrational state. These rules for conscious ascension weren't necessarily created by the Anunna, but they found ways of manipulating them to use for their benefit. The ultimate purpose of this tampering was to force human beings to exist in a state of energy and consciousness that they *don't* belong in.

This task of managing the energy cycles and balance on the planet was given to Enki, which is why he was "assigned" to the realm of the underworld. The Anunnaki assumed the role of gods to humanity since they consider themselves to be the original progenitors and parents of them. But were they really? Some would argue that what these beings did was unethical and wrong and that if left alone our species would have eventually reached this point on our own. My personal belief is that the truth is somewhere in between.

Just as the Nag Hammadi Scripture states in the chapter "The Hypothesis of the Archons," the Anunna became the "rulers of *our* reality," controlling how we perceive the world and universe around us. Consider for a moment the idea that another planet, similar to Earth, could exist in the galaxy that has another developing hominid species like us. Are they dealing with the same type of control and manipulation of their reality as we are? How common is this throughout the universe? As difficult as that may be to wrap your head around, it's certainly possible given how advanced they became on an interdimensional level.

This theory would also help to explain why they seem

to disappear from human history for thousands of years, existing beyond what we perceive as linear time. Perhaps that's why the Igigi are tasked with continuously monitoring humanity in the first place, to keep track of the changes here. On clear nights I often stare in humble amazement at the twinkling starlight from countless other star systems and planets and wonder, who else is looking back? Could they be asking the same questions that I am?

According to the laws that govern the universe, as well as our understanding of complex biology and planetary environments, I theorize that the development and evolution of an extraterrestrial species is heavily dependent upon the relative age of the star system they originate from. In general, the older that a star system is, the more potential it has for highly evolved and advanced civilizations to develop there. This is assuming, of course, that they didn't destroy themselves first. As these civilizations mature both consciously and technologically, their potential influence on the development and timeline of other less evolved societies greatly increases as well. Compared to most others around us, the Solar System we reside in is still considered relatively young.

Because of the powerful forces that govern duality in the universe, as well as the rules of free will, the human timeline has likely become interwoven with countless other sentient beings, not just the Anunnaki. Some of these beings, including the Anunnaki, could have potentially come from anywhere in the galaxy, or perhaps even *another* universe. This common interest shown towards Earth is largely fueled by the sheer importance of what humanity *could* become. This is what the cosmic struggle over free will is all about. With all this competition that exists around the outcome of Earth and the human race, the real question becomes, what lies ahead for us in the future?

Considering the enormous distances, time, and complexity needed to reach interstellar planets (known as space-time), it's only logical to surmise that a certain level of intelligence and technological sophistication is required to reach them. On a higher level, the more advanced beings become, the more inherent their responsibility becomes to positively influence others they encounter. That's why certain rules *must* be followed to allow the independent development of any sentient being. The bottom line is, if a society is ruled by the unsustainable mentality of war, conquering, and material gain for too long, eventually they will annihilate themselves. Only time will tell the direction that humanity will take and if we'll finally decide to seize control of our own destiny before it's too late.

Ancient Origins, Sirius, and the Dogon

Mesopotamian cuneiform tablets state that the Anunnaki referred to Earth as "Ki," which became an important soul incarnation planet for humans. These souls, such as you or me, could have potentially come from anywhere in the cosmos, and we shouldn't be so quick to define our origins to one single location in time and space. After all, consciousness resides on a multidimensional level. That's why the Earth is so important to so many of these sentient beings, as it's literally the "key" to the future. Think of humans as being eternal conscious creators, who are trapped in a physical body until they can grow and ascend beyond the third dimension. Unfortunately, due to certain circumstances, the deck has been largely stacked against us.

Some researchers theorize that the Anunnaki may be part of an ancient race of beings that are potentially *millions* of years old. This concept may be hard for some to wrap their heads around, especially considering the relatively short lifespans humans have *now*. However, according to the Sumerian King List, this may not have always been the case. The most important question becomes, where did these beings originally come from? We don't have a lot of concrete evidence, but there are clues, including the design of the Great Pyramid of Giza, the story of the Dogon and Nommo, and even the findings from Pioneer 10. I would like to point out at this time that some of this is based on pure speculation, but I still feel that the reader deserves to know that these possible connections exist.

The astronomical data gathered by Pioneer 10 provides compelling evidence to not only show that the Solar System is actually a binary star system, but that its history may greatly differ from what we've been told. So why is that important? The reason it's important is due to the specific wording that was used in the image shown in the 1987 *New Illustrated Science and Invention Encyclopedia, Vol. 18*, describing the discoveries made by Pioneer 10 which depicted the existence of a new planet, along with a dead star found more than 50 billion miles from Earth. I've shown this iconic image in several of my videos, and I highly encourage everyone to check those out.

The term "dead" star means that its potentially far

older than our Sun but has likely already lost much of its fusion core over time, becoming either a brown or red dwarf. This evidence supports the hypothesis that this dead star is part of what's called an invader solar system, that developed a long elliptical orbit after becoming trapped here millions to potentially billions of years ago. In fact, binary star systems are quite common in the galaxy and occur roughly 80% of the time.

Since this invader solar system is potentially far older than our own, it provides evidence to support the theory that Planet Nine may be somehow connected to the Anunnaki. Could this Ninth Planet act as a sort of outpost to observe the Solar System from afar? After all, the Igigi are commonly referred to in the Book of Enoch as "The Watchers" of Earth. However, despite this, I still don't feel that the evidence is conclusive enough to support Planet Nine being their place of origin. So then, if the Anunnaki didn't originate from Planet Nine, where could they have come from?

To answer this difficult question I've identified some key pieces of evidence which I feel helps to shed light on this area. The first piece of evidence comes from Mali, Africa with the Dogon tribe and their connection with the beings they called the Nommo, which I discussed in the previous chapter. When comparing the various depictions made of the Nommo, strong correlations can be found linking back to the Mesopotamian god known as Oannes, whose frequently portrayed wearing a type of amphibious fish suit. Based on this logic, it seems highly plausible that both Oannes and the Nommo are in fact the *same* being. This "fish suit" was largely seen as a symbolic representation for the Zodiac Age of Pisces, and was considered one of the original symbols held by Ea, who was later known as Enki. Eventually, this important symbol was adopted by the Christian church and turned into the religious Mitre Hat we still see worn by the Pope today.

When reviewing the explanations given by the Dogon people for how these beings arrived on Earth, they *clearly* state that they came from the Sirius star system, which is part of the Canis Major constellation. In fact, the Nommo even provided detailed descriptions of Sirius's three stars and their relative orbits in space. So how could a primitive tribe in western Africa have known these precise astronomical details without the use of a telescope? This would also have been especially difficult considering that Sirius C hasn't even been discovered yet. This evidence supports the hypothesis that some of the Anunnaki *may* be connected in some way to the Sirius star system, primarily those affiliated with Enki. This could explain why Enki has historically held a lower ranking among the Anunna than Enlil since he was only considered his half-brother.

Just as the Nommo imparted extensive knowledge about Sirius to the Dogon people, the ancient Egyptians also worshipped the same star system and even designed their early calendar system around its orbit. So then, the most important question is, where did the rest of the Anunnaki originate from? We may never actually know for sure, although some believe it could be connected back to the Orion constellation, or possibly even the Pleiades. Why else would these star systems be worshipped by so many cultures and civilizations throughout history? Was it just because of their fascination with energy cycles and the precession of the equinoxes? For now, many of the secrets contained within the Great Pyramid of Giza still remain somewhat of a mystery, but hopefully, in the future, more information will come to light that answers these difficult questions.

There will undoubtedly still be some individuals who read this book who feel there isn't enough evidence to support many of my theories and claims. To those naysayers, I point towards an unlikely source that many may have overlooked or simply not understood which I call "the big picture." In order to achieve this, one must develop an expanded awareness and comprehensive understanding of the fundamentals which govern our reality, and then have the ability to objectively separate out any unusual anomalies that don't correlate with the available evidence. Unfortunately, this usually means sacrificing a considerable amount of one's time to study and observation, which most don't have the ability or desire to do.

The most significant of these anomalies revolves around the specific means by which societies' perceptions of reality have been carefully manipulated for countless generations, creating a population who is largely governed by ignorance, blind nationalism, and misinformation. This is due to the fact that many have been taught through a greatly antiquated and inaccurate education system, that's heavily based on conformity and obedience rather than critical thinking and accuracy. Like a flock of sheep being endlessly led around in circles by a farmer, the version of reality we see today is the result of thousands of years of misinformation, conditioning, and war. Some may be wondering how exactly this proves outside intervention? Allow me to explain.

The sheer complexity by which our reality has been

carefully engineered around controlling the information surrounding history and religion, as well as consciousness levels, is *far* beyond the capabilities of any secret societies or powerful governments. They clearly help to maintain the status quo but aren't the original architects. Not to mention Mesopotamian cuneiform tablets clearly state that kingship, and the acquisition of knowledge regarding agriculture, laws, mathematics, and astronomy all originated from advanced beings or entities who reside in "heaven." How is it possible that cultures around the world just so happen to share the same symbols, knowledge, advanced building practices, and gods?

The only logical conclusion that makes sense to me is that mankind has been influenced by these "ordainers of destinies" from the *very* beginning. How else could human civilizations have acquired all of this knowledge so quickly over different time periods?

The Multiverse and the Stage of Time

In the end, the more one looks at the perfect rhythm and dance shared between light and dark energies, the more they begin to understand that the entire multiverse represents an infinite storyboard of possible timelines, all playing out on a grand stage according to the law of free will. In many ways, the human epic represents one of the *most* important stories of all since it has the potential to affect so much of the future. Despite the sheer boldness of that statement, many of the ancient texts from the past overwhelmingly support the importance of mankind finding balance and achieving higher states of energy, in order to finally reach the next stage of our conscious evolution.

However, I would like to point out that I fully recognize that the complexities of our history and the multiverse may be far too sophisticated to *fully* comprehend at this time. That statement isn't meant to cast doubt on the conclusions derived within this book, but rather to acknowledge the fact that we still have so much to learn about the nature of reality. But isn't that the point? The endless search to acquire knowledge and seek answers? Hopefully, someday, we'll collectively reach the level of consciousness needed where we can perceive our purpose and existence within the multiverse and leave behind the shackles of our limited awareness.

That's why it's important to remember that every action and decision we make contributes in some way to the direction that this great ship of human consciousness will take, as we wade through an endless sea of possibilities. Each person has the potential within themselves to change the entire course of history, becoming the heroes of our collective story, and allowing those accomplishments and sacrifices to echo for all of eternity. The way that *you* decide to spend your time is your choice. Will you spend it following a path dominated by darkness or light? In the end, it all comes down to how you'll use your precious *time* and energy here on this great *stage* of Earth.

Slowly step by step, humanity is embarking on a new chapter in its story, one that will hopefully illuminate the path towards Aquarius and pave the way for our infinite future. The true purpose of free will means that we *must* wander into the darkness to find our way back to the light. For without the wandering, there would be no catalyst to help us grow and change on a fundamental level so that we can finally transcend beyond the limits of time and space, to become creator gods of reality. (1,2,3,8,9,10,11,13,14,15,16,17,18,19,20,21)

Ancient Texts and Images Index

Ancient Texts Index

Images Index

Eagle and Serpent God's Name Table

Ea and Enlil

Human Civilization	Ea	Enlil
Sumerian	Enki	Enlil
Akkadian	Ea	Ellil
Persian	Ahura Mazda	Angra Mainyu
Greek	Prometheus	Zeus
Roman	Neptune	Jupiter
Nordic	Loki	Thor
Slavic	Veles	Perun

The Legacy of Thoth

Human Civilization	Thoth
Sumerian	Ningishzida?
Akkadian	Nabu?
Egyptian	Thoth
Atlantean	Thoth
Greek	Hermes
Maya	Kukulkan
Aztec	Quetzalcoatl
Inca	Viracocha?

Bibliography

1) Smith, George, "The Chaldea Account of Genesis", 1846, Henry Colburn, London.
2) Dalley, Stephanie, "Myths from Mesopotamia: Creation, the Flood, Gilgamesh, and others", 2000, Kensington Oxford University Press, Oxford.
3) Clark, Gerald R., "The 7th Planet Mercury Rising", Create Space Self-Publishing, 2013.
4) Doreal, "The Emerald Tablets of Thoth the Atlantean", Source Books, 1930, Gallatin, TN.
5) LaCroix, Matthew, "The Illusion of Us: The Suppression and Evolution of Human Consciousness, Create Space Self-Publishing, 2016.
6) Marciniak, Barbara, "Bringers of the Dawn: Teachings from the Pleiadians", Bear and Company, 1992, Rochester.
7) Sitchin, Zecharia, "The 12th Planet", Ishi Press, 1976, New York.
8) Pye, Lloyd, "Everything you Know is Wrong, Book One: Human Origins", iUniverse, 2000.
9) Plato, "Timaeus and Critias", Pantianos Classics, 1871, England.
10) Meyer, Marvin, "The Nag Hammadi Scriptures: The Revised and Updated Translation of Sacred Gnostic Text Complete in One Volume", HarperCollins, 2007, New York.
11) Hall, Manly P, "The Secret Teachings of All Ages", Penguin Group, 2003, New York.
12) King, L.W, "The Code of Hammurabi", Lillian Goldman Law Library, 2008, Connecticut.

*All internal images are either license-free from the public domain or taken by the author

Credits

Barbara Marciniak (1), David Icke (2), Graham Hancock (3), Dr Steven Greer (4), Zecharia Sitchin (8), Michio Kaku (9), Lloyd Pye (10), Robert Bauval (11), Robert Schoch (12), Randall Carlson (13), Mark Passio (14), Gerald Clark (15), Michael Tellinger (16), George Smith (17), Stephanie Dalley (18), Manly P. Hall (19), Brien Foerster (20), Robert Temple (21)

ABOUT THE AUTHOR

Matthew LaCroix is a passionate writer and researcher who grew up in the outdoors of northern New England. From an early age, a strong connection back to nature was established and built into the morals of his life. His persistent yearning for adventure led him into profound, life-changing experiences that inspired him to write for local and national magazines such as Backpacker and AMC Outdoors.

While attending Plymouth State University, he published his first book at the age of 22 and began studying history, philosophy, quantum mechanics, and superstring theory. His focus became uncovering and connecting the esoteric teachings from secret societies and ancient cultures that disappeared long ago. At 32, he published his second book, *The Illusion of Us*, which combined years of research to discover the truth about the past, human origins, as well as the fundamentals of consciousness.

In 2019, he released his third book entitled, *The Stage of Time*, which represents a compilation of ancient texts, spiritual wisdom, and theoretical physics, combined together to answer some of our most difficult questions. From understanding the complexities of reality, to lost history, and the identity of the gods of antiquity, no stone is left unturned in the endless pursuit of truth.

CPSIA information can be obtained
at www.ICGtesting.com
Printed in the USA
LVHW091450290720
661854LV00001B/87